Wissenschaftliche Beiträge aus dem Tectum Verlag

Reihe Politikwissenschaft

Wissenschaftliche Beiträge
aus dem Tectum Verlag

Reihe Politikwissenschaft
Band 81

Andreas Schwenk

Finding a Cue through "Q"

Applying Q-Methodology to Compare German and U.S. Diplomats' Attitudes towards U.N. Security Council Reform

With a foreword by Prof. Dr. Steunenberg

Tectum Verlag

Andreas Schwenk
Finding a Cue through "Q". Applying Q-Methodology to Compare German and U.S. Diplomats' Attitudes towards U.N. Security Council Reform
Wissenschaftliche Beiträge aus dem Tectum Verlag
Reihe: Politikwissenschaft; Bd. 81

ISBN 978-3-8288-4306-6
E-PDF 978-3-8288-7239-4

Umschlaggestaltung: Tectum Verlag unter Verwendung des Bildes
545765479 von Gareth Lowndes | shutterstock.com

Printed in Germany

Besuchen Sie uns im Internet
www.tectum-verlag.de

Bibliografische Informationen der Deutschen Nationalbibliothek
Die Deutsche Nationalbibliothek verzeichnet diese Publikation in der Deutschen Nationalbibliografie; detaillierte bibliografische Angaben sind im Internet über http://dnb.d-nb.de abrufbar.

Foreword

The study "Finding a cue through Q" focuses on how people communicate and whether they share similar perceptions the moment they engage in negotiations. For decision-making studies, this understanding is quite crucial. In her article 'An agenda for the study of institutions', published in 1986, the Nobel prize winner Elinor Ostrom sketches how decision-making is embedded in a broader context. It includes structural as well as institutional characteristics, which shape the outcome of decision-making. While decision-making is often reduced to simply a calculus of costs and benefits, a richer institutionalist approach also includes normative components. People may not only decide on what they like, but also how possible outcomes link with deeper values such as fairness, equality or something alike. And these values matter when it comes to deciding on an important but difficult issue.

In this book, the reform of the UN Security Council is such an issue. It is a difficult one: years of discussion and debate have preceded current discussions. Already in 1992 reform was put on the political agenda. It is an important issue: the discussion determines whether and how the UN may act, on behalf of its members, in case of various international conflicts. Andreas Schwenk carefully reconstructs these debates and the various reform proposals since then. As this study shows, reform continues to be an issue of various opinions and approaches with yet the common goal to find a workable solution for the future.

In order to analyze the current process, Schwenk uses Q-methodology to assess the normative points of view, but also judgements, contentions and capabilities of these actors. Q is a qualitative methodology to identify discourses through a careful collection, scoring and analysis of a broad and diverse set of statements, which are part of the overall discussions on some topic. Discourses are used to understand why negotiators are not able to find an acceptable solution.

Based on the analysis in this book, two discourses appear to be present in current debates. One is the discourse of convinced institutionalism. In this discourse, the UN Security Council is perceived as an institutional body in which geography and member state contributions should be part of the degree of control individual members have on decision-making. The other discourse is cautious institutionalism. Any change of the existing structure would be, in this discourse, a risky enterprise gambling with world peace and security. Therefore, any change of the current (veto) structure should not be made. While sharing agreement on the institutional identity and role of the council, both discourses prominent among the interviewed diplomats from Germany and the United States, differ in their assessment of risk and opportunity ahead.

The study is a nice example of how differences in normative understanding affect the outcome of decision-making. The study also nicely shows how the extensive discussion on reforming the UN Security Council is stalled. Only a geopolitical disruption changing the interest perception of the council members, or a step-by-step reform process with temporary trial periods for new council formats, would allow for progress.

I would like to wish you a lot of pleasure in reading this book. I am confident it will provide you with further insight in a complex but very interesting debate.

Bernard Steunenberg
Leiden University
6/2/2019

Abstract

United Nations Security Council reform has been an issue on the agenda of the United Nations once again since the end of the Cold War, and the following realignment of power structures in the international system. While the debate about reform has been intensively held until about 2007, reform efforts have stalled since then. In this master thesis, I attempt to seek possibilities for a revival of said debate through a combination of political discourse analysis and intensive Q-Methodology in search of common ground. For this study, diplomats from the Federal Republic of Germany and the United States of America were included as participants. They were asked to rank statements out of the two countries' discourses on UN Security Council reform according to agreement or disagreement. Instead of presenting study participants with a priori categories, this method allows me to reconstruct typologies for dominant discourses, based on the answers of the study participants. Social perspective narratives were then created for the results, leading to the surfacing of the dominant discourses. In this study, two different discourses were discovered in an analysis of the study participants' rankings: 1. Convinced Institutionalism & 2. Cautious Institutionalism. The results of this study can be used to relate UN Security Council reform to political discourses in the two countries on this subject, further clarifying positions from a cross-national comparison.

Table of Contents

1. Introduction

The United Nations Security Council constitutes the most crucial organ of this international organization founded in 1945, carrying the security- and military-related responsibility of the United Nations. After the devastation of World War II and the preceding failure of the League of Nations, the international community came together to create a lasting international organization to maintain international peace and stability. According to Article 24 of the United Nations Charter, the Security Council holds "primary responsibility for the maintenance of international peace and security", which is conferred on it by the members of the United Nations. Thereby "in carrying out its duties under this responsibility the Security Council acts on their behalf" (UN Charter, Ch. V, Art. 24, Para. 1). The Security Council "shall act in accordance with the Purposes and Principles of the United Nations" (UN Charter, Ch. V, Art. 24, Para. 2) and the members of the United Nations "agree to accept and carry out the decisions of the Security Council in accordance with the present Charter" (UN Charter, Ch. V, Art. 25). Chapters VI, VII, VIII, and XII of the UN Charter then furthermore lay out the details according to which the council may exercise the specific powers granted to it in cases such as the "settlement of disputes" (UN Charter, Ch. VI), "action with respect to threats to the peace, breaches of the peace, and acts of aggression" (UN Charter, Ch. VII), "regional arrangements" (UN Charter, Ch. VIII) and the "international trusteeship system" (UN Charter, Ch. XII).

At its founding in 1945, the Security Council was made up of eleven members of which five were the so-called permanent ones and six were the so-called non-permanent ones. In 1965, the council was enlarged to fifteen members, which has been the only structural reform in its history. Following this, the current council still exists and operates within the structures of 1965. Nowadays, it is made up of fifteen members of which five are the so-called permanent ones and ten are the so-called non-permanent ones. The five permanent members are made up of the five victorious nations of World War II: The People's Republic of China, the French Republic, the Russian Federation (formerly the Union of Soviet Socialist Republics), the United Kingdom of Great Britain and Northern Ireland, and the United States of America. These five countries have been represented on the council continuously since 1945 and are vested with a veto right to block any resolution on the council which might not be in their interest. The ten non-permanent members are selected by their regional groups for two-year terms on a rotating basis. Within the United Nations, there are five regional groups. After the UN's founding in 1945, the groups were: 1. British Commonwealth; 2. Eastern Europe & Asia; 3. Latin America; 4. Western Europe; 5. Middle East. During the reform of 1965, the groups were changed into the following: [1. African Group; 2. Asia-Pacific Group; 3. Eastern European Group; 4. Latin American & Caribbean Group; 5. Western European & Others Group]. This group scheme still persists today in the same way as the 1965 Security Council scheme persists today. Each of the five groups nominates members for a two-year term. In contrast with the permanent members, the ten non-permanent members have no veto rights on the council. A security council resolution is passed when nine out of the fifteen members vote in favor and none of the five permanent members uses a veto.

The set-up of the security council has been at the receiving end of critique throughout most of its existence with certain countries feeling under-represented on the body or not sufficiently vested with rights such as the veto. After the end of the Cold War, this critique has intensified. The main reasons for this intensification are the demand for an updated version of the council's structure, adequately reflecting the new geopolitical realities of the post-Cold War world and the 21st century. Since the council's founding, France and the United Kingdom seem to have lost their world power status, while Russia is no longer a super power after the fall of the Soviet Union. The immediate post-Cold War world of the 1990s has left the United States as the only remaining super power in a largely unipolar world order. The 21st century predicts the rise of China as a new world power to challenge this unipolarity. Russia's role and the role of the two European countries remain unclear. Furthermore, globalization has diversified the influence and weight of the world, adding more countries to the picture.

While nowhere near as powerful as the world's current only superpower, the likes of India and Brazil have been gaining international importance in the recent years. On the European continent, Germany appears to re-emerge as a player, steering the Eurozone through its financial troubles and increasingly gaining political relevance globally as well. The European Union, while experiencing some hick-ups at the moment, has achieved greater harmonization among European countries over time and increasingly acts as a single player. All of this opens the question to whether the current Security Council set-up still reflects the balance of power of the 21st century and thus, whether another reform of the council's structure is necessary.

The reform of the United Nations Security Council is a topic that leaves a huge space for creativity and wishful thinking, but also for constructive progress and thoughtful reform proposals. Several reform proposals out of the diplomatic and academic world have emerged in the last 25 years since the end of the Cold War with none of them having reached a true breakthrough. From the diplomatic proposals of the Secretary-General's High-level Panel Report (2004), the "G-4"[1] (2005), the group "Uniting for Consensus"[2] (2005), the "African Union"[3] (2005) or the "S-5"[4] (2006) to the various academic works of Joseph Schwartzberg (2004; 2005; 2007; 2013), the analysis of Kara McDonald and Steward Patrick (2010), the critiques of Maurice Bertrand (1985) or the analysis of Richard Butler (2012), the topic of council reform has sparked immense interest and a great amount of contributions.

This master thesis will engage in a comparison of diplomats' attitudes from the United States of America and the Federal Republic of Germany on UN Security Council reform. Diplomats are selected purposefully, as they have inside knowledge on the process from the perspective of their two respective countries. The two countries are of particular interest for a comparative study, as they belong to two different categories within the reform effort. The United States being one of the United Nations' founding members and current veto power, belongs to

1 Group of Four: Brazil, Germany, Japan, India.
2 Uniting for Consensus: Argentina, Canada, Colombia, Costa Rica, Italy, Malta, Mexico, Pakistan, Republic of Korea, San Marino, Spain, Turkey.
3 African Union: All member states.
4 Small 5 Group: Costa Rica, Jordan, Liechtenstein, Singapore, Switzerland.

the category of countries that hold permanent seats (P-5), while Germany being one of the most commonly mentioned aspirant countries belongs to the category seeking a permanent seat in a potential reform. While in theory many other countries could have been incorporated in such a comparative study, I decided to use these two for reasons of most convenient access to information, and language fluency in both English and German. Due to personal contacts, it was easier for me to establish contacts to the diplomatic services of these two countries than it would have been to any other countries. Furthermore, attitudes among the two countries' diplomatic services might serve as a check-up of congruence in foreign policy goals with the United Nations, as well as the current state of affairs of the "transatlantic bridge". With its growing economic importance and de-facto leadership role in the European Union, Germany appears to have become an ever more important partner for the world's only remaining superpower, the United States. Close cooperation between these two countries on a UN-level contributes to stability, peace and security in the world, and is thus a corner stone for both nations' foreign policies. A renewed look at the potential for cooperation in "taking the United Nations into the 21st century" between two such crucial UN-member states could prove of utter importance, especially after recent reform efforts have stalled. Possible room for maneuvering, as well as findings of policy congruence might aid in a reinvigoration of the debate on UN Security Council reform for the benefit of both countries.

2. Literature Review

2.1. Two Countries in the United Nations Security Council

2.1.1. The Federal Republic of Germany

After World War II had left Germany in ruins, immediate popular attention was not given to foreign policy or the United Nations, but much rather to more elementary tasks of reconstruction and livelihood. Germany's preliminary legal status had only been enshrined in 1949 with the founding of the Federal Republic of Germany [West Germany] and the German Democratic Republic [East Germany]. The so-called "enemy-states articles" of the United Nations Charter (UN Charter, Ch. VIII, Art. 53; UN Charter, Ch. XII, Art. 77; UN Charter, Ch. XVII, Art. 107) provided that any potential action taken against Germany would not be subjected to its otherwise binding rules. As these articles prevented Germany from becoming a full member of the United Nations, it resorted to an observer status without any voting rights, similar to what the Holy See and Palestine hold today. The Hallstein Doctrine (1955)[5] made sure that East Germany did not become an observer state until the 1970s, as West Germany effectively was able to block the United Nations from recognizing the East. The enforcement of this doctrine ended with the introduction of Chancellor Willy Brandt's Ostpolitik, eventually leading to full UN membership for both German states in 1973. The enemy-states articles were declared obsolete by the United Nations General Assembly in 1995, but remain in the charter.

5 The Hallstein Doctrine declared the official recognition and establishment of diplomatic relations by third-party states (except the Soviet Union) with the German Democratic Republic as an "unfriendly act". As it was in the interest of other western states to isolate the East, an official UN membership application by East Germany was prevented. Similar circumstances in diplomacy can still be found today in the People's Republic of China's "One-China Policy" with regards to Taiwan.

Germany has been elected to an overall five times to a two-year non-permanent seat on the United Nations Security Council. The first time came only four years after its admittance to the organization for the period of 1977–1978 as West Germany, during which the country played an active role in Namibia's independence preparations. East Germany served as a member once during the period of 1980–1981. West Germany's second term came for the period of 1987–1988, which was also supported by the East. After reunification in 1990, West Germany took over the dissolved East, now having one seat for the reunified country. The next Security Council term followed for the period of 1995–1996 with an increased role and status in the international arena. The 21st century has seen two terms so far during the periods of 2003–2004 and 2011–2012, being overshadowed by disagreements in the council on the Iraq War and the Libya no-fly zone respectively (DGVN, 2016). During the most recent period, Germany was especially active, creating multiple draft resolutions on the situation in Syria and the Arab Spring, which failed due to the resistance of veto powers Russia and China (Auswärtiges Amt, 2014). In 2016, Germany announced that it will campaign for another two-year non-permanent term for the period of 2019–2020 (Auswärtiges Amt, 2016).

The German quest for a permanent seat on the United Nations Security Council can be followed in a progressive matter from 1990 onwards, becoming ever more pressing. In the first years after reunification, calls for a permanent German seat on the UN Security Council were not present, as the struggles of the reunification process and the dawning first Gulf War were too dominant (Hellmann, 2007). Furthermore according to a speech by former German Foreign Minister Genscher (1990), German foreign policy should, out of responsibility for the European continent, follow a multilateral European approach without pure national Machtpolitik. After two world wars having been initiated by Germany, the concern over any German claims for its own seat was still too great. In addition, Germany did not want to prove British and French doubts over the consequences of German reunification right. The strongest claim was a suggestion by former Chancellor Brandt (1990) that Germany should share the two permanent European seats with France and the United Kingdom. When Klaus Kinkel became the new foreign minister in the early 1990s, he still relatively shyly formulated a wish for a German seat, but made clear that no unilateral initiative would be taken (Kinkel, 1992). In a statement by the German Federal Government on the issue the following year, the term "natural candidate" was coined for the first time (Bundesregierung, 1993). According to Hellmann, et al. (2007) the position showed that Germany saw itself as a natural candidate based on its economic power, but instead of claiming its own right to a seat, was pressed for it by others due to its increased importance. Any reference to a sharing agreement of permanent seats with France and the United Kingdom had disappeared. In the coalition contract of the new German Red-Green government in 1998, a claim for an own seat was reiterated, if the quest for a European seat fails (Coalition Contract, 1998). In a speech by foreign Minister Joschka Fischer (2004) before the Bundestag, the word "if" suddenly became the word "because". Germany had apparently come to the conclusion that a failure of a European seat was clear and it should therefore pursue solely its own seat. What followed in 2005, was a draft resolution (United Nations, 2004) put forward by the so-called Group of Four, consisting of Brazil, Germany, India and Japan on a concrete reform proposal.

Since German reunification, the country has seen a progression on its position for an own UN Security Council seat from a wish to a claim. This claim is supported by five factors: economic strength, international expectations and responsibility, German national interest, legitimacy, and multilateralism (Hellmann, 2007). Germany's relatively large economic output as the world's fourth biggest economy (International Monetary Fund, 2016) and large contribution to the United Nations as the third biggest contributor after the United States and Japan with 7.141% of the budget, (United Nations, 2015) builds a strong case for a permanent seat. Former German Permanent Representative to the United Nations Gunter Pleuger (2003) stated that the expectations of the international community have grown especially since German reunification. As a now post-Cold War, reunified and extremely wealthy developed state, Germany should take more responsibility for and in the world than it has done before as a political dwarf. In terms of national interest, a raised profile with more influence would yield greater possibilities for Germany to shape the world according to its wishes. To do so in the UN Security Council would constitute principal capabilities in one of the most important organizations of the world. The German expectation should be to "take responsibility within the process of globalization" and to incorporate a "role" that gives the possibility for "encompassing contributions" (Pleuger, 2003, 688). For the fourth factor of legitimacy, it is to be said that an inclusion of more broadly geographically distributed member states as permanent members of the UN Security Council, as well as the inclusion of the biggest contributors to the UN budget would raise the legitimacy of the council. For the last factor of multilateralism, Pleuger (2003) states that part of the international demands for Germany to take up more responsibility in the world is the conviction that it is a trustworthy multilateralist. In an interview for this master thesis, former German ambassador Doris Hertrampf called Germany a "Zivilmacht" (civil power), taking reference to precisely this assumption.

In an analysis of Germany's last term on the UN Security Council, Gowan (2013) introduces two myths about German foreign policy: the myth of German strength and the myth of German weakness. These two myths present two opposing interpretations of Germany's foreign policy behavior during the 2011–2012 term, marked by the country's abstention on the Libya no-fly zone issue. While on some occasions such as in Afghanistan or at the Horn of Africa, Germany remains aligned with its western allies, on other issues such as the Libya abstention it sided with the BRIC-countries. The myth of German strength interprets the abstention as an assertion of Germany's new power on the international stage and a realignment of its foreign policy towards a more independent position, sometimes siding with western countries and sometimes with non-western countries. This realignment stems from a new confidence among Germany's political elite in terms of being able to independently steer its own foreign policy. The myth of German weakness on the other side interprets the reaction to the abstention as a sign of a failed attempt to steer Berlin's foreign policy independently and thus sees a retreat back to the traditional western allies.

Whichever one of these two myths might be or might not be reality, Germany's candidacy for its sixth non-permanent term for the period of 2019–2020 shows a continued willingness to fulfill its role in the world through the UN Security Council. Besides Germany's willingness to contribute and to shape, the country's continued commitment to Security Council reform stays an official part of its policy towards the United Nations. Former German ambassador Doris Hertrampf assured that her country seeks an honest discussion on a feasible and just reform. Germany has distinguished itself as a cooperative leader in the world since reunification. German foreign policy is based on arguments and convincing strategies, rather than on coercion or force. This is a key in organizations such as the United Nations. In another interview for this master thesis, former German Permanent Representative at the United Nations Dr. Gunter Pleuger agreed with this assessment, stating that Germany indeed does not even have any Machtpolitik anymore.

2.1.2. The United States of America

The United States of America is a founding member of the United Nations having emerged as one of the victorious states out of World War II. Inspired by its predecessor, the League of Nations, the United Nations was founded at the United Nations Conference on International Organization in San Francisco in 1945 by 50 participating countries. Since then, the United States has held its permanent seat enshrined in the UN Charter, thereby being one of the permanent five (P-5) members of the UN Security Council. Due to the veto status of both the United States and the USSR, the Security Council found itself in a deadlock on any issue directly or indirectly related to Cold War policy between the two opposing sides. This situation remained the case until the formation of the post-Cold War order in the beginning of the 1990s. The first sign of the newly found decisiveness in the Security Council were Security Council Resolutions 687 and 688 (1991) requiring Iraq to abandon its arsenal of weapons of mass destruction and establishing a no-fly zone over Iraq respectively. The United States led a coalition of countries to respond to the Iraqi invasion of Kuwait in 1991. After a short period of decisiveness, described by then UN Undersecretary-General Brian Urquhart as a "false renaissance" (Meisler, 1995), a backlash occurred with multiple crises during the 1990s to which the Security Council was unable to find solutions. During the years of the Clinton Administration, the UN Missions to Somalia, to Bosnia and to Rwanda were viewed as failed, since all were unable to prevent widespread killings or even genocide. The NATO-led intervention in Yugoslavia in 1999 was not approved by the Security Council. Neither was the 2003 intervention in Iraq during the Bush Administration prior to which then US Secretary of State Colin Powell attempted to convince council members of the presence of weapons of mass destruction. Nevertheless, two years earlier in 2001, Security Council Resolution 1386 (2001) established the International Security Assistance Force [ISAF] in Afghanistan as a response to the terror attacks on the World Trade Center in New York City of the same year. While since the end of the Cold War, the UN Security Council has continued to enjoy authority and legitimacy in US foreign policy, the world's only superpower seems to reserve the right for itself to act without the body's approval, where deemed necessary.

In terms of the positions of the United States on the reform of the UN Security Council, no concrete proposal has ever been outlined. Instead, the United States concentrates on responding to proposals brought forward by aspirant countries, and setting a lose set of criteria for membership. Support for certain aspirant countries over others has changed over time. In a paper by the US Department of State (1999), "the United States supports a strengthened and expanded Security Council, including permanent seats for Germany and Japan", while "there should be no change in the status or privileges of the existing permanent members" (US Department of State, 1999, 52). In 2003, the State Department introduced seven principles for UN reform, including "responsibility, accountability, effectiveness, stewardship of financial resources, modernization, credibility, and freedom". Furthermore, the United States "stressed that any Security Council reform must focus on practical, achievable reforms to enhance its ability to effectively implement its original mandate" (US Department of State, 2003, 136–137). In 2004, US policy on Security Council reform included that it must "be supported by a broad consensus" (US Department of State, 2004, 124) of member states. The themes of effectiveness and efficiency in any reform of the United Nations seem to be of particular relevance to the United States. Especially in the aftermath of the 2003 Iraq invasion, the effectiveness and efficiency of the United Nations was widely doubted. Thus, in 2005 the US Congress created a task force jointly chaired by former Speaker of the US House of Representatives Newt Gingrich and former Senate Majority Leader George Mitchell. This report published through the United States Institute of Peace came to roughly the same conclusion as the prior mentioned US State Department papers, stating that any potential expansion of the council must "enhance its effectiveness and should not "detract from the Councils efficiency and ability to act in accordance with the UN Charter." (US Institute of Peace, 2005, 7). Following the task force's criticism on the overall mismanagement of the United Nations, the United Nations Reform Act (2005) passed by the US House of Representatives demanded that the US contributions to the UN budget should be reduced by 50% if no improvements would be made by 2008. The 2010 US National Security Strategy of the Obama Administration comes to yet again a familiar conclusion of UN Security Council reform, stating that any potential reform should be one that "enhances the UN's overall performance, credibility, and legitimacy" (The White House, 2010, 46).

In a report for the Council on Foreign Relations, McDonald and Patrick (2010) summarized the situation at hand and gave recommendations for future U.S. policy in the area. Responding to criticisms on the lack of legitimacy of the UN Security Council, the two authors take a legal perspective stating that the sole legitimacy of the council comes from the UN charter created in 1945. They choose to refer to article 23 (1) of the UN Charter, arguing that the council does not have a legitimacy problem. Since geographical distribution of the membership is mentioned as a secondary factor, the ability to contribute to enduring peace and security is the primary one. Equal distribution among the UN's regional groups therefore is of lesser importance for council membership than the power to be a guarantor of world peace. This power may be of military, economic, diplomatic or technological nature. Furthermore, the continuous involvement of the UN Security Council in kinds of matters of international conflict shows the authority and legitimacy it has in the eyes of the member states. Nevertheless, the two authors argue that council reform is in the "enlightened self-interest"[6] (McDonald & Patrick, 2010, 10) of the United States. By taking a pro-active role in shaping the reform debate, the United States could construct any potential reform in its favor. The two authors recommend a combination of a criteria-based approach and a long-term approach. The criteria-based approach would include a "history of political stability", a "globally or regionally deployable military", "financial contributions to the UN regular budget", "financial contributions to UN peace-keeping operations", and a "demonstrated willingness to use, when appropriate [...] sanctions, force, international intervention" (McDonald and Patrick, 2010, 21). The long-term approach recommended by the two authors would include a proposal for an interim permanent seat on the UN Security Council, as well as the increased importance of aspirant states in other international organizations to prove their willingness and capability to shoulder the burden.

Taking a different approach on the question of legitimacy Lyman (2000) sees an immense lack of legitimacy of the UN Security Council, as "for much of the world, the Security Council is seen as unrepresentative, biased, and increasingly ineffective". In addition, many members accuse it of applying a "double-standard" when selecting where to send peace-keeping troops or humanitarian aid, as well as especially the United States for its policy position on the International Criminal Court[7] (Lyman, 2000, 2). Lyman (2000) suggests reforming the UN Security Council in a way that 75% percent of the world's GDP and between 57% and 63% of the world's population would be directly represented.

---

6 McDonald and Patrick take reference to a term created by John Ikenberry (2001) in his book "After Victory: Institutions, Strategic Restraint, and the Rebuilding of Order after Major Wars". Ikenberry describes that victorious powers tend to create strong institutional frames in their favor to lock other states in. Examples of this would be the Peace of Westphalia (1648) ending the 30 Years War, the Concert of Europe at the end of the Napoleonic Wars (1815), the League of Nations after World War I (1920), and the United Nations after World War II (1945).

7 The United States signed the Rome Statute of the International Criminal Court, but the US Congress has never ratified it. Therefore, the United States is a party to the statute, but not obliged to enforce it. Practically, this means that the United States can support and/or encourage cases over war crimes, crimes against humanity or genocide against individuals of other states, but US individuals would not be subjected to this.

The overall US position on UN Security reform has not dramatically changed since the beginning of the post-Cold War period. One shift in 2003 was to remove its support of Germany as a candidate. The US's main interests are to keep the council effective and efficient, while at the same time maintaining its power share. The first interest would mean that a heavy enlargement of the council is not in the interest of the United States, as more members would make consensus more difficult. The second interest would mean keeping the status in terms of the veto, while including as many allies as possible in any potential enlargement. Bosco (2015) argues that while the status-quo is possibly the best option for the United States, a limited reform should nevertheless be in its interest to appease the emotions around Turtle Bay. He proposes adding six new semi-permanent seats to the council without veto rights. Semi-permanent according to him would be a four- or five-year term with the possibility of a re-election. He claims that the great part of this plan is that nobody would be completely satisfied, but everybody could live with it. In an interview for this master thesis, former US Ambassador Richard Boucher stated that the optimal outcome for the US would be simply adding the Group of Four [Brazil, Germany, India, Japan] plus one African country to the council, making them permanent without a veto right.

2.2. Main Initiatives and Draft Resolutions

When the topic of UN Security Council reform was put on the agenda again in 1992 after the last reform in the 1960s, General Assembly Resolution A/RES/47/62 (1992) was a first milestone taken on the road to a new Security Council reflecting the realities of the post-Cold War world. The resolution invited all members to bring forward suggestions on how the Security Council should be reformed. The following year, a report drafted by the then UN Secretary General Boutros Boutros-Ghali summarized the results of the member states proposals, leading to General Assembly Resolution A/RES/48/26 (1993). This resolution established the so-called "Open-Ended Working Group", whose task it was to lay out a detailed report on realistic reform scenarios for the future of the Security Council. Four years later in 1997, the so-called

Razali Paper (1997)[8] named after the Open-Ended Working Group's Chairman Ismail Razali was submitted to the General Assembly. Resistance came in 1998 with General Assembly Resolution A/RES/53/30 (1998), reminding member states of the necessity for a two-third majority for any change to the Security Council structure. After Security Council reform was also a topic in the United Nations Millennium Summit in the year 2000, the UN High-level Panel Report (2004)[9] gave further detailed recommendations on Security Council reform. Building on and interpreting this report, four different draft resolutions were distributed in the UN General Assembly: draft resolution A/59/L.67 (2005) by the African Union, draft resolution A/59/L.64 (2005) by the Group of Four, draft resolution A/59/L.68 (2005) by the group Uniting for Consensus and draft resolution A/60/L.49 (2006) by the group Small Five. These four draft resolutions together with the High-level panel report form the basis of reform proposals until today. After more than a decade of stalling negotiations within the setting of the Open-Ended Working Group, member states decided to move to a different forum in 2007. With General Assembly Decision 62/557 (2008) member states moved to a forum of intergovernmental negotiations between single states and the groups that had already been formed in the prior process. This new setting is called the Intergovernmental Negotiations (IGN). Decision 62/557 (2008) sets the most pressing issues of Security Council reform out as: (A) the different categories of membership, (B) the veto, (C) regional representation, (D) enlargement of the council and working methods, (E) cooperation between the Security Council and the General Assembly. In the following years, negotiations have centered around different set-ups and term arrangements. Some of these are recommendations on being more flexible with terms for seats on the Security Council. Longer terms for some seats, short terms with the possibility of a re-election or longer non-permanent terms that evolve into permanent seats are some examples. However, no new breakthroughs have been reached and the negotiations have

8 Paper by the Chairman of the Open-Ended Working Group On The Question of Equitable Representation and Increase in the Membership of the Security Council and Other Matters Related to the Security Council.

9 A more secure world: our shared responsibility – Report of the High-level Panel on Threats, Challenges and Change.

stalled. The most current effort to reinvigorate the debate came with Populated Framework Document (2015) in which 120 member states expressed their views on reform prospective once again.

2.2.1. The "Razali Reform Paper"

After UN General Assembly Resolution A/RES/48/26 (1993) had established the Open-Ended Working Group, requesting an assessment of reform outlooks and a written report, the group began its work under the chairmanship of Malaysian diplomat Ismail Razali. The "Razali Reform Paper" was the result of the group's assessment, culminating in a working paper. This working paper was the first serious new reform proposal since its first reform in 1965. As requested, the paper outlined the group member's consensus on potential reform scenarios of the UN Security Council. The "Razali Reform Paper"[10] (1997) was distributed in the General Assembly on December 3rd, 1997, after four years of deliberations on the subject matter. It suggested increasing the size from fifteen to twenty-four members, adding five permanent seats and four non-permanent seats. The distribution of permanent seats was envisioned to be in the following pattern: developing states of Africa (1), developing states of Asia (1), developing states of Latin America and Caribbean (1), industrialized states (2). The seat distribution of non-permanent seats was supposed to be: African States (1), Asian States (1), Eastern European States (1), Latin American and Caribbean States (1). Noteworthy in this reform proposal is that for the new permanent seats, the countries are not divided along the lines of the UN's regional groups, but along the lines of developing and developed states. Only in the category of non-permanent seats, there is a return to the regional group division. On the issue of the veto power, the "Razali Reform Paper" discourages its use, limiting it solely to matters covered by Chapter VII[11] of the UN Charter. Simultaneously, it de-

10 Paper by the Chairman of the Open-Ended Working Group On The Question of Equitable Representation and Increase in the Membership of the Security Council and Other Matters Related to the Security Council.

11 Action with respect to threats to the peace, breaches of the peace, and acts of aggression.

cides that the new permanent members of the Security Council shall have no veto rights. The affirmative vote on the new 24-member council shall be at fifteen, requiring amendments to article 27 (2) and (3) of the UN Charter. The report also decides to amend article 53 of the charter, by deleting any reference to former enemy states[12] and to eliminate article 107[13] accordingly. Furthermore, the paper calls for transparency enhancing measures, such as an increase in regular meetings with non-members of the council, monthly consultations with the General Assembly and regular briefings on the council's progress to non-members.

2.2.2. The High-Level Panel Report

When at the United Nations Millennium Summit in September of 2000 leaders of member states came together to what was the then "largest gathering of world leaders in history" (BBC News, 2000), deliberations on the role of the UN in the 21st century were on the agenda. What came out of this gathering was the United Nations Millennium Declaration with the Millennium Development Goals[14]. All leaders back then agreed to help the populations of the poorest parts of the world to feel a real improvement in their every-day lives by the year of 2015. The UN Millennium Declaration was divided into the points (1) Values and Principles, (2) Development and Poverty Eradication, (3) Protecting our Common Environment, (4) Human Rights, Democracy and Good Governance, (5) Meeting the Special Needs of Africa, (6) Strengthening the United Nations (United Nations, 2000). The issue of Security Council reform was briefly touched upon in the last aspect [Strengthening the United Nations] as "to intensify our efforts to

12 "The term enemy state as used in paragraph 1 of this Article applies to any state which during the Second World War has been an enemy of any signatory of the present Charter." (Article 53 [2], UN Charter)

13 "Nothing in the present Charter shall invalidate or preclude action, in relation to any state which during the Second World War has been an enemy of any signatory to the present Charter, taken or authorized as a result of that war by the Governments having responsibility for such action." (Article 107, UN Charter)

14 http://www.un.org/millenniumgoals/

achieve a comprehensive reform of the Security Council in all its aspects" (United Nations, 2000).

Four years after the dissemination of the UN Millennium Declaration, a report by the so-called "High-level Panel on Threats, Challenges and Change" was distributed as a follow up to the declaration together with UN General Assembly Presidential Note A/59/565 (2004). The High-level report (2004) was attached under the title "a more secure world: our shared responsibility". The at that time UN Secretary-General Kofi Annan entrusted former Thai Prime Minister Anand Panyarachun with the chairmanship of the panel. The panel's task was to "assess current threats to international peace and security; to evaluate how our existing policies and institutions have done in addressing those threats; and to make recommendations for strengthening the United Nations so that it can provide collective security for all in the twenty-first century" (United Nations, 2004, 1). Threats identified by the report were (1) poverty, (2) infectious disease, (3) environmental degradation, (4) inter-state war, (5) civil war, (6) genocide, (7) other atrocities, (8) weapons of mass destruction, (9) terrorism and (10) transnational organized crime.

Part of this report was a proposal on a reform of the UN Security Council. The report says that a future council should not simply be made representative covering all the regional groups equally, but should be kept as a "responsible body able to take decisive action" (United Nations, 2004, 79). Expansion should not solely be based on "geographical balance but also on contributions to maintaining peace and security" (United Nations, 2004, 80). Any reform, according to the report, should increase the effectiveness and credibility of the council without undermining its readiness to act. It should also make it more democratic and accountable, broadening its membership especially to the developing world. The member states contributing the most to the UN budget should be given preference when being elected for council seats. Contributions can be of financial, military or diplomatic nature to the objectives and mandates of the United Nations. The report does not give a specific reform recommendation, but presents two models for member states to consider. The first reform present in both models is a reorganization of the current regional groups. The group "Western European and Others" would be split up. Western Europe would be merged with the Eastern European group to make it one "European Group". The remaining "others" would also be merged with different groups. The United States and Canada would join the group "Latin American and Caribbean", making it the "Americas". Australia and New Zealand join the Asian group, making it "Asia-Pacific". Thus, the group number would be reduced from five to four with the new regional groups being (1) Africa, (2) Americas (3) Asia-Pacific, (4) Europe. Therefore at the status-quo, Africa would have no permanent seats, the Americas would have one, Asia-Pacific one and Europe three. According to the report, the Security Council is to be enlarged to twenty-four members with each of the four new regional groups having six seats. Distribution Model A introduces six new permanent seats without the right of a veto and three new non-permanent seats for two-year terms. Africa and Asia-Pacific would receive two permanent seats respectively, Europe and the Americas would receive one seat respectively. This would bring the total count of permanent seats up to eleven with only the original five having veto powers. Africa would have two permanent seats without veto powers, Asia-Pacific would have three permanent seats [one with veto power & two without veto power], the Americas would receive two permanent seats [one with veto power & one without veto power] and Europe would have four permanent seats [three with veto power & one without veto power]. Furthermore, Africa would receive four spots for non-permanent seats, Asia-Pacific would receive three such spots, the Americas would receive four and Europe would receive two. This would divide the council into an eleven permanent seats [five with veto power & six without veto power] and thirteen non-permanent seats to an overall of twenty-four. Distribution Model B introduces no new permanent seats at all, instead creating a new category of non-permanent seats. The new category would be a renewable four-term for which all regional groups would receive two spots. In addition in the two-year non-renewable category for non-permanent seats, Model B proposes awarding four new seats to Africa, three new seats to Asia-Pacific, three new seats to the Americas and one new seat to Europe. This would bring the seat distribution to five permanent seats with veto power, eight new renewable four-year term non-permanent seats equally distributed among the regional groups and eleven non-renewable non-permanent seats. Model B would also have an overall of twenty-four seats on the Security Council.

Regional area	*Number of States*	*Permanent seats (continuing)*	*Proposed new permanent seats*	*Proposed two-year seats (non-renewable)*	*Total*
Africa	53	0	2	4	6
Asia and Pacific	56	1	2	3	6
Europe	47	3	1	2	6
Americas	35	1	1	4	6
Totals model A	191	5	6	13	24

Regional area	*Number of States*	*Permanent seats (continuing)*	*Proposed four-year renewable seats*	*Proposed two-year seats (non-renewable)*	*Total*
Africa	53	0	2	4	6
Asia and Pacific	56	1	2	3	6
Europe	47	3	2	1	6
Americas	35	1	2	3	6
Totals model B	191	5	8	11	24

Both models are designed to encourage member states to contribute more resources to the UN budget by potentially rewarding them with longer or renewable seats. The report furthermore states that this should not be the last reform, as with ever-changing times, the need for another reform may arise in the future. It accentuates that in neither model, a new veto power would be created, as the authors see "no practical way of changing the existing members' veto powers" nevertheless calling the institution as such "anachronistic" (United Nations, 2004, 82).

2.2.3. The Group of Four

The Group of Four is a group of countries made up of Brazil, Germany, India and Japan. The four countries cooperate within the field of UN Security Council reform by publicly supporting each other's bids for a permanent membership. They base their aspirations for this membership on the strength of their economies as well as on the growing political weight of their voices in a world in which the balance of power is shifting away from US-dominated unipolarity to an increasingly diversified power share. Furthermore, the relatively high financial contribution to the UN Budget is raised as another argument in favor (Auswärtiges Amt, 2016). Economically speaking, it is especially Germany and Japan that have come out of the Cold War as winners and 25 years onwards continue to be in relative good economic shape. Germany is Europe's de-facto economic leader, while Japan remains Asia's second biggest economy after China. Both countries currently rank 3rd and 4th according to the nominal gross domestic products figures of the International Monetary Fund (2016). In a New York Times (1990) opinion piece, John Ullmann, a professor of management at Hofstra University, called the two countries the actual winners of the Cold War, because they have not wasted their resources on an arms race, but followed more wise and long-term oriented policy approaches. India and Brazil being the other two members of the Group of Four, are two more additions to the world's more diversified power share. As the world's largest democracy in terms of population size, India has consistently grown its economy and developed into a regional power in the possession of nuclear weapons. Brazil, even though experiencing some recent economic trouble fueled by corruption scandals in the government of Dilma Rousseff and wide scale administrative mismanagement (The Economist, 2016), has positioned itself to be a leader in South America. The four countries of this group make up the most likely choices for UN Security Council expansion, as they in addition to the economic strength and political weight, have been voted to the council as non-permanent members for 64 years cumulatively since the UN's founding. This length shows an overall trust in the countries by the rest of the UN's member body.

On July 6th, 2005, a draft resolution was brought forward in the UN General Assembly by a group of countries centered around the Group of Four, calling for a reform of the council by enlarging it and by extending the veto right to a greater number of member states. Draft Resolution A/59/L.64 envisions an expansion of the UN Security Council from 15 to 25 members with four non-permanent ones and six permanent ones being added. The four non-permanent members shall be one African state, one Asian state, one Eastern European state and one Latin American and Caribbean state. The six permanent members shall be made up of two African states, two Asian states, one Latin American and Caribbean state and one Western European and Others state. It is obvious that the states being considered are the members of the Group of Four plus two African states of which the contenders are Egypt, Nigeria and South Africa. In the argument of the initiators, this draft resolution constitutes a fair consideration of the regional distribution of new members, increasing the council's legitimacy in the eyes' of member states. Furthermore, effectiveness and credibility would be increased through a more representative council, reflecting current world realities. In addition, the draft resolution aims at greater transparency of the council's working methods through regular briefings of non-members from the General Assembly. On the issue of the veto, the draft resolution states that the six new permanent members shall not exercise their right until a review of the new situation created by the draft resolution has been undertaken fifteen years after.

On September 29, 2015, the four members of the Group of Four reiterated their aspirations in their latest joint press release on the topic, stating that a "more representative, legitimate and effective Security Council is needed more than ever to address the global conflicts and crises, which had spiralled in recent years." (Bundesregierung, 2015).

2.2.4. The Group "Uniting for Consensus"

The group "Uniting for Consensus" [nicknamed "Coffee Club"] was formed in 1995 under the leadership of Italy as a response to the aspirations of the G-4. As can be deducted from the group's name, its aim is to reach a consensus among UN member states prior to making any decision on an actual reform effort. The group opposes any expansion of permanent seats, but instead advocates for an overall enlargement of non-permanent seats from ten to twenty (Ariyoruk, 2005). It was especially former Italian Permanent Representative to the United Nations Franscesco Paolo Fulci, who even after his official assignment ended, stayed longer in New York City for other UN functions to continue advocating privately. Notably so, it can be said that among the group members of the "Coffee Club" one can find expected regional competition from the regions of the G-4. Italy here would serve as the counterpart to Germany, Colombia and Argentina as counterparts to Brazil, as well as Pakistan and South Korea as counterparts to India and Japan.

One draft resolution from 2005 and one further proposal from 2009 have been brought forward by the group "Uniting for Consensus", where the proposal serves as a supplement to the initial draft resolution. Draft Resolution A/59/L.68 (2005) includes an increase of the seats for non-permanent members from 10 to 20, making the council one of 25 members overall. The draft resolution does not call for any expansion of the permanent membership, but aims at further visualizing the divide between veto powers and non-veto powers by simply increasing the latter. Furthermore, greater space for regional rotation for members from the five regional groups would be enabled, creating a more equitable geographical distribution. The twenty non-permanent members are to be elected to the pattern of African States (6), Asian States (5), Latin American and Caribbean States (4), Western European and Others States (3), and Eastern European States (2). Whether a direct re-election after a fulfilled two-year term is possible shall be decided upon by each of the five regional groups for their own members. An affirmative voting majority shall be reached at fifteen out of twenty five votes with no veto-power objecting. The draft resolution also calls for improved consultation between the Security Council and the General Assembly and the Economic and Social Council. To make these changes possible, article 23 (1) and (2), article 27 (2) and (3), as well as article 109 (1) will have to be amended.

The major differences to prior efforts in the most recent proposal from 2009 (Global Policy Forum, 2009) is the creation of a completely new category of seats on the Security Council. In addition to the traditional 2-year non-permanent seats, two new alternative categories are put forward. Either an additional 2-year category shall be created, whose members would be re-electable or a completely new category of 3- to 5-year terms shall be created. A further difference between these two categories is that members in a 2-year term will have the possibility of a re-election, while the 3- to 5-year seat does not hold this possibility. The longer term seats will also be allocated to regional groups on a partly rotational basis as follows: African States (1), Asian States (1), African/Asian States (1 – rotational basis), Latin American and Caribbean States (1), Western European and Others States/Eastern European States (1 – rotational basis). The original 2-year non-permanent terms without the possibility of a re-election would be upheld with the following allocation: Small States[15] (1), Medium-Sized States[16] (1), African States (1), Asian States (1), Latin American and Caribbean States (1), Eastern European States (1). The majority required for passing resolutions on the Security Council is set at 15 out of 25 member states. For the veto right, two options are given: either a complete abolition or a limitation to the usage of the veto to an inter-alia application limited to Chapter VII of the United Nations Charter: "action with respect to threats to the peace, breaches of the peace, and acts of aggression". Lastly, the proposal calls for a review of the mechanism after a period of either 10 to 12 years or 15 to 16 years, taking into consideration the terms of the seats and a comprehensive reassessment of the working methods and composition.

2.2.5. The African Union

After having been largely ignored in the power struggles and negotiation rounds of the UN Security Council during much of the second half of the 20th century, African countries have started an attempt to increase their chances at their own permanent seats in the early 21st century as well. In the Ezulwini Consensus (2005)[17], a common African position on the proposed reform of the United Nations focus-

15 Member states with a population of less than 1 million.
16 Member states with a population of between 1 million and 10 million.
17 The Common African Position On The Proposed Reform Of The United Nations – "The Ezulwini Consensus"

ing on international peace and security matters, was formed. The Ezulwini Consensus covers various topics ranging from famines, poverty and debt management, international trade, environment concerns, inter- and intra-state armed conflict, the elimination of nuclear weapons, UN sanctions enforcement, peace-keeping missions, nation building, and the institutional reform of the United Nations itself. All of these issues are combined and framed as collective security problems for the African continent. Considering the aspect of United Nations Security Council reform, the Ezulwini Consensus demands at least two permanent African seats and five further non-permanent seats. The consensus was adopted by the African Union in March 2005. Facing significant opposition to the number of demanded seats in the UN General Assembly, the Sirte Declaration (2005) was adopted by the African Union in July of the same year. The Sirte Declaration scales down Africa's demands from five non-permanent seats on the council to two non-permanent seats. Both the Ezulwini Consensus and the Sirte Declaration form the basis on which the African attempt for Security Council reform is based.

On July 18th, 2005, the African Union countries distributed their own draft resolution for Security Council reform in the UN General Assembly. Draft Resolution A/59/L.67 calls for expansion of the council size from the current fifteen to an overall of twenty-six members, creating eleven new seats. The seat distribution for new permanent seats in the African proposal would be as follows: African States (2), Asian States (2), Eastern European States (0), Latin American and Caribbean States (1), Western European and Others States (1). The seat distribution for new non-permanent seats in the African proposal would be as follows: African States (2), Asian States (1), Eastern European States (1), Latin American and Caribbean States (1), Western European and Others States (0). An important factor distinguishing the African resolution is that it demands the same derogatives and privileges for the new permanent members, including the veto right without any reassessment after a certain time period.

With three non-permanent seats for Africa at the current set-up of the UN Security Council, but no permanent seats, Africa has a lot to gain in any potential reform scenario. While the African Union is currently demanding two permanent seats and two non-permanent seats, it is questionable whether an argument for more than one permanent seat will be accepted by non-African countries. On the African continent itself, there are three potential candidates for the permanent seats. These potential candidates are Egypt, Nigeria and South Africa. Therefore, Africa is in a competition for two (most likely one) seats with three aspirant countries. While the first candidate has been politically extremely unstable in recent years following the resignation of former President Hosni Mubarak during Arab Spring and the events on Tahrir Square against military rule and Mohamed Morsi, the other candidates don't look that much better. Nigeria is in the midst of the fight against Boko Haram. Furthermore, to quote former British Prime Minister David Cameron, it is "possibly one of the most corrupt countries in the world"[18] (The Guardian, 2016). South Africa is riddled in its own domestic governance problems under President Jacob Zuma and still suffering from the effects of an unfinished societal process after the Apartheid regime ended in 1994.

2.2.6. The "Small Five"

Another reform initiative for the United Nations Security Council was brought forward by a group that formed in 2005. The group is called the "Small Five" and consists of Costa Rica, Jordan, Liechtenstein, Singapore and Switzerland with the latter being the unofficial leader. The group's name is supposed to work as a metaphor for being the exact opposite of the "Big Five" (permanent member of the Security Council with a veto power). In an effort to increase the inclusiveness and transparency of the council's working methods, this group calls exclusively for a greater incorporation of small member states into the council's work. A statement by the former Swiss Permanent Representative to the United Nations Mr. Peter Maurer backs this by stating that only a few member states will benefit from an enlargement of the council, but

18 Former UK Prime Minister David Cameron called Afghanistan and Nigeria "fantastically corrupt" and "possibly two of the most corrupt countries in the world". He made those remarks in a verbal conversation at the 2016 London Anti-Corruption Summit with the Archbishop of Canterbury Justin Welby, the Speaker of the House of Commons John Bercow and Queen Elizabeth II of England.

the great majority would only benefit from improved working methods. All UN-member states that contribute to peace-keeping missions should receive a greater overview of the Security Council's plans, as they are expected to share the burden of the enforcements of United Nations missions (Schweizerische Eidgenossenschaft, 2009).

In draft resolution A/60/L.49 (2006), the group suggests interactive and informal discussions between the Security Council and the General Assembly. Furthermore, special subject-oriented reports by the Security Council to the General Assembly on issues of international concern such as peace-keeping missions or sanction enforcement shall be drafted. In addition, more substantive exchanges of views between the Security Council, the General Assembly and the Economic and Social Council shall be held. Regular and timely consultations between members and non-members of the council shall be held as well. On the use of the veto right in the Security Council, the group "Small Five" suggests that all members making use of this right should have the obligation to explain themselves in a written document issued to all council members. The veto shall not be used in the event of genocide, crimes against humanity and serious violation against international humanitarian law. While the draft resolution was never officially put up for a vote, some suggestions on consultations and transparency have later been taken up in a Presidential Note issued by the Security Council (S/2006./507, 2009). In an interview given to the British Broadcasting Corporation (BBC News, 2012), Mr. Peter Maurer called this "a significant achievement" and "a step in the right direction" (Schweizerische Eidgenossenschaft, 2009). Up until today, the suggestions of the group "Small Five" have however not become part of the council's standard procedures.

2.3. An Academic Approach: The "Schwartzberg Reform Proposal"

A completely different approach to United Nations Security Council reform comes from the academic world. Professor Joseph E. Schwartzberg is a professor emeritus in geography at the University of Minnesota, who came up with a totally different and very parliamentary solution to the problem. Being a member of the World Federalist

Movement[19], Professor Schwartzberg favors a model for the United Nations that reflects the relative position of one member state compared to all others. In his academic proposal and analysis "Revitalizing the United Nations: Reform through Weighted Voting" (Schwartzberg, 2004) he developed a system of weighted voting in which every UN member state will have a voting weight according to its international position in relation to the rest. Schwartzberg's main point of critique of the current voting system of the United Nations is that each country has one vote with the exact equal weight. The system of "one state – one vote" does not reflect the realities of the balance of power in the world, which should be taken into account at UN votes as well. In the current system, Micronesia's vote in the General Assembly has the same weight as the one of the United States. As one can imagine, this has been a point of critique by the more powerful member states since the UN's founding and was only acceptable to them through the introduction of the veto right in the UN Security Council (Council on Foreign Relations, 2015). Professor Schwartzberg (2004) wants to reform the current system of "one state – one vote" by replacing it with a method of weighted voting. He developed a specific formula for this weighted vote: "(P+C+M)/3". In his formula, "P" stands for the percentage of the member state's population among the UN membership, "C" stands for the percentage of the member states' financial contributions to the UN budget or alternatively the member state's gross national product's percentage compared to all others, and "M" stands for the member state's unit share among the UN's membership. Then, the result is divided by three to get the average of the three prior factors.

Schwartzberg (2004) wants to apply this system to the UN General Assembly primarily. In the setting where each vote counts the same, now the countries' votes would carry a certain percentage weight. According to his formula, the five UN member states with highest weighted vote in the General Assembly would be: (1) United States [9.064% in contributions OR 11.716% in GNP], (2) China [7.672% in contributions OR 8.462% in GNP], (3 OR 4) India [5.960% in contributions OR 6.3455 in GNP], (3 OR 4) Japan [7.282% in contributions OR 5.423% in GNP], and (5) Germany [3.835% in contributions OR

19 World Federalist Movement-Institute for Global Policy. http://www.wfm-igp.org/

2.987% in GNP]. For the UN Security Council, Professor Schwartzberg (2004) envisions an expansion of the council from fifteen seats to a maximum of eighteen seats with the veto right having been eliminated. This number is based on calculations he has made in his work. All member states with a contribution or GNP percentage of at least 4% would be guaranteed a permanent seat. According to his formula, this would only apply to the four highest ranked countries of the United States, China, India and Japan. Simultaneously, he would dissolve the current UN regional groups that are entrusted with selecting candidates for non-permanent seats. Instead, he would allow all member states to freely choose their group affiliations and also allow groups to change. As one will only be able to have a seat on the UN Security Council with a contribution or GNP percentage of at least 4% and most members will want to have a seat, Schwartzberg (2004) expects member states to start sharing seats in newly formed, like-minded groups. The new groups could then be formed according to economic, security, cultural, linguistic, religious, etc. connections among member states. In all of these circumstances, a maximum of eighteen different regional groups would emerge. These groups of like-minded could then choose their representatives, acting as groups on the council. Schwartzberg (2004) predicts that this move would eliminate the fierce competition among members of the same regional groups, as now only like-minded countries would come together. Some of his group suggestions include the (1) Arab League; (2) Central Europe; (3) Central, Easter and Southern Africa; (4) China; (5) Eastern Europe; (6) India; (7) Japan; (8) Meso-America; (9) Non-Arab Islamic States of Central and Southwest Asia; (10) North Atlantic Bloc; (11) Northern Europe; (12) South America; (13) Southern Europe; (14) Southeast Asia; (15) United States; (16) Western Africa; (17) Western Europe.

2.4. Assessment of Main Initiatives

The mentioned literature has shown a great depth of reform suggestions for the UN Security Council coming from both official policy proposals and UN documents, as well as from the academic world. From the Razali Paper and the UN-High Panel Report to the reform proposals of the Group of Four, the group "Uniting for Consensus", the African Union, the group "Small Five" or the Schwartzberg reform proposals, suggestions for institutional reform are plenty. The remaining question however is, whether some of those are practical and feasible.

The classical interpretation of the situation found on the UN Security Council is reflected by game theory, as each negotiating player must fear to suffer consequential losses. The losses to be suffered in the debate on council reform would be to either not be included in the way aspired or to not be included at all. For a P-5 veto power such as the United States, an abolition of the veto would constitute a catastrophic reduction of the bargaining power on the council, while an extension of veto powers to further states would constitute a relative reduction. Aspirant states such as Germany would be able to increase their bargaining powers with either an acquired veto power or an enlargement of the member size of the council. However, aspirant states are also put against each other, as further aspirant countries such as Italy might not be considered in the veto discussion. The crux of the matter remains a lack of trust or assurances within the international system that one state will in fact live up to its promises. Might Germany remain a strong partner for the United States within the western alliance if it acquires a veto? Might Germany remain a proponent of pan-EU ideas, also taking into consideration Italian interests once it has a veto? Can the United States rest assured that an extension of the veto and enlargement of the council will not detract from the Security Council's effectiveness? None of these questions can be answered prior to a real-life simulation. The problem is that the post-simulation status cannot be reversed once it has been instated. In terms of bargaining power on the UN Security Council, Winter (1996) has shown that a crucial part is time. According to him, bargaining power of the non-veto states on the council is basically zero, as any decision can be stopped at any time by the veto powers. An attempt was made with the first reform of the UN Security Council in 1965 to undermine the P-5's bargaining power enlarging the council from eleven to fifteen, but this would have only been successful without the veto. With the veto as it stands, the first reform had no effect. Neither would a second reform with no change to the veto have any effect to the said bargaining power of the P-5. A mere enlargement to 25 members would not change anything. An extension of the veto to other states would give more states the same absolute bargaining power, but discrepancy to non-veto states would remain unchanged. Winter (1996) therefore argues that the only reform aspect to relativize the absolute bargaining power of the veto states, would be to put a time limit on the decision-making process. However, the limit would have to have the consequence of a loss for everybody. If a situation arises out of whose continuation all veto powers would suffer harm, the bargaining power of the veto is diminished. Should environmental policy and climate change policy ever be framed in terms of security, this might become interesting in council negotiations. As climate change affects everybody equally, negotiation delay through the veto power would become nonsensical. Therefore, the bargaining power of non-veto states would be increased. On the other side, without the time limit, the P-5 continue to have absolute bargaining power. This serves as yet another proof for George Tsebelis's (2002) veto player theory, arguing that the outcome of policy in any legislative body is dependent on veto players within it. Using rational-choice institutionalism, this theory claims that the outcome of policy depends on "(1) the number of veto players, (2) the distance between these players' policy ideal points, and (3) the players internal cohesion" (Wirkola, 2010, 3). Tsebelis (2002) explains that the existence of an area between the veto players' ideal policy preferences preserves the status-quo on a policy. He calls this the "unanimity core". In the case of the United Nations Security Council, a further core is the "qualified majority core", which is needed as resolutions are passed with a 9/15 majority. The case of the P-5's absolute bargaining power therefore remains for reform negotiations of the council, as can be see in the accusation of a "delaying strategy" by German Ambassador Hertrampf (Ret.). Hosli et al. (2011) continue with the deliberation on bargaining power by adding the potential for winning coalitions to the conversation. Analyzing the effectiveness of the decision-making process and the weighted-voting power of member states, they use the Coleman Index of the power of a collectivity to act. In the first structural period of the UN Security Council (1945–1965), the collective weight of the veto powers' voting power stood at 90.48% and in the second structural period (1965–present) at 83.46%. The Coleman Index for decision probability stood at 2.78 and

2.59 respectively. In the event of an enlargement following the proposal of the Group of Four (of which Germany is a member), the collective voting power of the then ten veto powers in an enlarged 25-member council would be 62.53% with a Coleman Index for decision probability of 1.84. This means that while the overall weighted-voting power of the member states with a veto power would decrease, winning coalitions would also become more difficult to find. Thus, one can expect the use of the veto in the UN Security Council to become more frequent under any enlargement scenario, supporting US Ambassadors (Ret.) Wood and Boucher's concern for council ineffectiveness. With reform negotiations having stalled however, the UN Security Council remains a structured institution whose equilibrium is the rules of the status-quo (Shepsle, 2005).

3. Methodology

After a multitude of various reform proposals and differing policy opinions between Germany and the United States on UN Security Council reform, it is the intention of this master thesis to evaluate where common ground is to be found nevertheless. This shall be done by a comparative approach. As the issue of UN Security Council reform is one widely discussed amongst policy experts and public officials in both countries, clearly held opinions on the subject matter can be expected. For this master thesis, ten diplomats (five Germans & five Americans; both active and retired) were chosen to participate in a sorting of Q-samples to evaluate their attitudes towards UN Security Council reform. The methodological approach chosen for this thesis was "Q-Methodology", which is a very useful scientific approach to evaluate opinions or attitudes within smaller, but more relevant, directly related and influential groups (such as diplomats for foreign policy issues) to deduct tendencies in larger populations. The normal sample size for participants within this method ranges between 10 and 50 (Müller et al., 2004, 3). "Q-Methodology" is therefore not meant to be representative in terms of the sample size of participants used, intentionally concentrating on a limited field of experts to find typologies among qualified opinions or attitudes.

As a mixture of quantitative and qualitative research methods, "Q-Methodology" is a useful tool to identify and evaluate subjective attitudes or opinions of individuals. In particular, it aids in the assessment of individuals' preferences to be put in relation to each other. With the help of typology creation, the participants' attitudes on the subject matter are than compared to each other. "Q-Methodology" was first published by psychologist and physician William Stephenson (1935) in his article *Correlating Persons Instead of Tests* and further elaborated on in detail in *The Study of Behavior: Q-Technique and Its Methodology* (Stephenson, 1953). While traditional "R-Methodology" in social science (i.e. political surveys) relies on a priori created categories into which participants are grouped, "Q-Methodology" is reconstructive (Dryzek et al., 1993). In this methodological approach it is precisely the results of the participants' answers that create the categories, and not the researchers defining the categories for the participants. In the end, this methodology does not compare "patterns across variables, but rather patterns within and across individuals" (Dryzek et al., 1993, 50). "Q-Methodology" finds itself as a very popular scientific approach throughout various fields of social science. It is especially in political science (Baas, 1997; Brown, 1980; Dryzek et al., 2000; Richard, 2000; Thomas, et al., 1996), medical psychology (Chen, 1996; Kogan et al., 2002; Lecouteur et al., 2001), media studies (Carlson et al., 2001; Singer, 1997; Singer et al. 1996), market research (Byung et al., 2001; Mosyagina et al., 1997), environmental psychology (Barry et al., 1999; Shilin et al., 2000); and gender studies (Febbraro, 1995; Gallivan, 1994) that "Q-Methodology" has left a scientific impact. In "Q-Methodology", the researcher selects an array of statements to be put forward to the study participants just like in a regular survey. A set of statements is called a Q-Sample, which is then ranked by the study participants according to for example their agreement with the statement from "-5" (do not at all agree) to "+5" (absolutely agree). According to Müller et al. (2004), there are three categories of statements: naturalistic statements, ready-made statements, and standardized statements. Naturalistic statements were made by the study participants themselves through news releases, publications or speeches. Ready-made statements come from the "life context" (Müller et al., 2004, 6) of the participants. Standardized statements are taken from standardized personality tests. The sample design of a "Q-Methodology" study can be either theoretically structured or theoretically unstructured. In a theoretically unstructured design, the statements are randomly reduced to Q-Samples. In a theoretically structured design however, the statements are reduced into Q-Samples by categorizing them with the intent of equal categorical representation. The results of each participant after the study process are then referred to as Q-Sorts, meaning that the participant has ranked the reduced set of statements (Q-Sample) according to his preferences (Q-Sort). There are two ways of allowing the participants to rank the Q-Samples. One way is to have unforced Q-Sorts, which means that for example on a scale of "-5" (do not agree at all) to "+5" (absolutely agree), the participant is allowed to put as many statements as he wishes into each ranking strength. Another way is to have forced Q-Sorts, which means that the participant is limited to a certain number of times he can put statements into a particular ranking strength. All the prior is the normal process and is referred to as an extensive Q-methodological analysis. In addition to this, there is the intensive Q-methodological analysis, in which the researcher choses to take a more intensive look at some participants through, for example, interviews.

For this master thesis, the "Q-methodology" approach was combined with political discourse analysis as found in Dryzek et al. (1993), and the conducting of additional interview rounds with some diplomats. An overall of 150 statements were collected out of various sources from the German and American discourses on the topic of UN Security Council reform to be able to formulate a reflection of the discourse on said topic at hand in both countries. The statements are both naturalistic and ready-made. These statements were collected from official policy documents (32), press briefings (17), magazines (27), government reports (13), academic papers (26), international treaties (23), and online journals (12). For the reduction process of the statements to transform them into Q-Samples, a theoretically structured design was chosen as in Dryzek et al. (1993). The categories chosen were in accordance with Seidel's (1985) and Alker's et al. (1986) essential elements of political discourse: (1) ontology; (2) agency; (3) motivation; (4) natural relationship. According to Dryzek et al. (1993), an ontology is a "set of entities recognized as existing", an agency is an institution "assigned to these entities", a motivation is the reason that drives the agent's behavior, and natural relationship refers to "hierarchies taken for granted" (Dryzek et al., 1993, 51). Furthermore to make it two dimensional, the political discourse elements were put against different types of claims. As one can expect within political discourse, claims about the world will be made. Therefore, four types of claims were selected in accordance with Toulmin (1958). These four types of claims are: (1) definitive; (2) designative; (3) evaluative; (4) advocative [see Table 1]. Definitive describes the definition or meaning of something, designative describes a question of fact, evaluative concerns the value of something, while advocative deals with something that could or should exist. All 150 statements from the primary selection process were then grouped into the created matrix according to the prior introduced categorization into one of the 16 cells. A statement from cell 2 for example is "When the Security Council legislates, it sets rules for the United Nations membership as a whole." One from cell 7 is "Germany has in all its decisions on the Security Council always taken into account EU interests." Another statement from cell 9 reads "Every modification of the veto will meet substantial resistance from the side of the five permanent members." One more statement from cell 16 is "Membership of the Security Council shall be increased from fifteen to twenty-four by adding five permanent and four non-permanent members."

Table 1
Matrix for Sampling a Concourse

	Discourse Elements			
Type of Claim	Ontology	Agency	Motivations	Natural
Definitive	1	2	3	4
Designative	5	6	7	8
Evaluative	9	10	11	12
Advocative	13	14	15	16
Note: Numbers indicate the cells from 1 to 16.				

From each of the cells, two statements were selected on being the farthest away from each other in their meaning. Through this process, the original 150 statements could be reduced to an overall Q-Sample of 32 out of 16 categories with two statements per category. The Q-Sample of 32 statements was then presented to the ten participants of this study, five American diplomats and five German diplomats. In addition, interviews were conducted with some study participants to be able to reflect on the results in a more detailed way. Therefore, this study constitutes an intensive Q-methodological approach. The participants were asked to rank the statements on a scale from "-4" (completely disagree) to "+4" (completely agree) with a voting strength of "1; 2; 4; 5; 8; 5; 4; 2; 1" [see table 2]. The reason for why diplomats were exclusively chosen as study participants is due to their expertise on the subject matter

(UN Security Council reform) and international relations as a subfield of political science, their insight on their countries' respective policies vis-á-vis the United Nations, and their knowledge about internal deliberations of the two respective diplomatic services on the subject matter. After collecting all the Q-Sorts of the study participants, a principal component factor was performed. Following, the factors were rotated within a varimax factor analysis. Lastly, a Q-Analysis was performed. All three statistical calculations were performed with Peter Schmolck's[20] PQMethod 2.35 software[21][22].

Table 2
Scoring Sheet

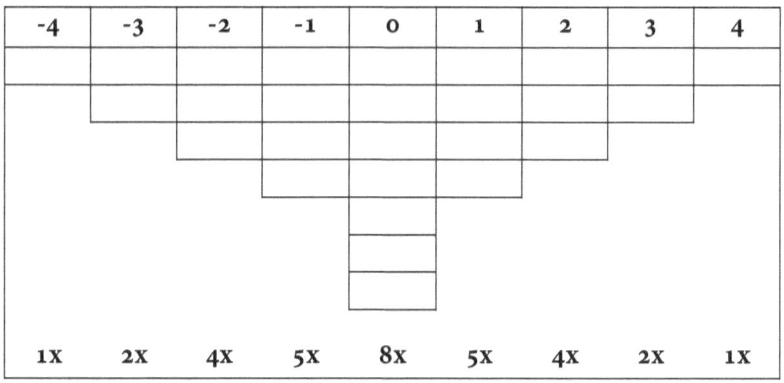

-4	-3	-2	-1	0	1	2	3	4
1x	2x	4x	5x	8x	5x	4x	2x	1x

20 Peter Schmolck, M.A. is a former scientific research assistant at the Bundeswehr University Munich. http://schmolck.userweb.mwn.de/

21 http://schmolck.userweb.mwn.de/qmethod/.

22 The original FORTRAN software is called Qmethod, and was developed by John Atkinson at the Kent State University in 1992 for mainframe platforms.

4. Results

4.1. Analysis of Interviews[23]

For this master thesis, various interviews were conducted with diplomats from Germany and the United States. Four of the various interviews were conducted with retired diplomats. Two of the interviewees are former US diplomats, while the other two are former German diplomats. On the American side, Ambassador (Ret.) Richard A. Boucher and Ambassador (Ret.) William Braucher Wood agreed to interviews. On the German side Ambassador (Ret.) Doris Hertrampf and Ambassador (Ret.) Dr. Gunter Pleuger agreed to interviews. While conversations with active diplomats from both sides were held during the preparations for this thesis, it is noteworthy to say that on neither side, any active diplomats agreed to be quoted or referred to in this thesis. A comparison of the four interviews held with retired diplomats showed that prior official policies from UN documents and discussions in journals or magazines were echoed. The diplomats did not seem to have any radically new approaches to the issue of UN Security Council reform, and both sides seemed to be rather pessimistic. US Ambassador (Ret.) Boucher stated that reform efforts have gone nowhere and that reform might even be farther away than ten years ago. German Ambassador (Ret.) Hertrampf even said that she does not expect any change to the status-quo by 2030. While both American and German diplomats were pessimistic on the future success of any reform, reasons for the current gridlock differed between the two sides. Ms. Hertrampf was of the opinion that the United States was not interested in reform, because it feared a loss of power. Therefore, the US was follow-

23 The statements made by the retired diplomats in the interviews conducted for this master thesis do solely reflect the personal opinions held by the interviewees. In no way are they reflective of, or to be associated with, the official policies of the two countries in this study.

ing an avoiding strategy by intentionally provoking a never-ending debate. Boucher instead raised concern over the disagreement between aspirant countries making reform impossible. Germany wants an honest discussion, according to Hertrampf, but according to Boucher, every country had its own reasons for why it should be on the council, and yet nobody could agree on whether those were the right reasons. US Ambassador (Ret.) William Wood stated that reform was just not operational, as there is too much disagreement before even getting to the P-5 states. In terms of the veto right, there was expected disagreement between the two sides as well. While both Hertrampf and Pleuger agreed that an enlargement of the Security Council would only be possible with new veto powers, Boucher and Wood said that any new vetoes would be a non-issue. Boucher commented that ideally he preferred a "5+5+5" solution[24], in which there would the the current P-5 together with five permanent members from the G-4 proposal without a veto, plus five non-permanent members. Pleuger however stated that with every further year of the status-quo, the veto power would be delegitimated. Another interesting aspect was the difference in the two sides' interpretation on the council's legitimacy. Wood saw its legitimacy coming from the authority enshrined in it by the UN Charter. The P-5's capability to ensure world security and peace plays an important role here. Boucher questioned whether Germany's military would have the capability to fulfill this role. Pleuger on the other side saw legitimacy coming from the representativeness of the council. The question of the German military becoming more powerful again was described as a dilemma for the country, according to Hertrampf. Thus, for Wood there is no lack of legitimacy for the Security Council, while for Pleuger the lack of representativeness causes a lack of legitimacy. The greatest future concern that was raised from the German side was that with the status quo continuing, the UN might become irrelevant. As more countries deem the set-up of the Security Council to be unreflective of the 21st century, more solutions to world problems might be looked for in different settings. While the German side seemed to bemoan such a potential development, Wood said that he

24 [China, France, Russia, UK, US] permanent with veto + [African State, Brazil, Germany, India, Japan] permanent without veto + [Five regionally selected states] non-permanent without veto

would welcome solutions from all settings, also from outside the UN. The greatest future concern on the US side was that a potential reform might undermine the council's effectiveness. According to Wood a reform that would make the council parliamentary would be a bad idea. A 25-member council should be the absolute limit.

A potential step forward to making the UN Security Council more reflective of the 21st century was given by the two US diplomats in the form of the EU sharing its two permanent seats. However, a sharing between France and Germany was preferred to the UK joining such an agreement. For all Europeans this seems to be out of the question. Another idea might be a permanent seat for the European Union, for which the UN Charter would have to be amended. While the German diplomats continued to argue for institutional reform, to make it more legitimate, their US counterparts suggested Germany should concentrate its efforts on other issues not in gridlock. According to Wood, Germany is part of the solution for world problems, not part of the problem. Germany's voice is loud and clear, and the country should continue to use its influence to make positive changes. UN Security Council reform however, remains unlikely.

4.2. Two Typologies

Through a close study and interpretation of the factor correlations and Q-analysis used in this study, one "unipolar" and one "bipolar" (Webler, et al., 2009) factor can be identified. Each of the two factors are resembled by an idealized, theoretical Q-sort which was calculated. The two idealized Q-sorts are referred to as factors A and B [see table 3]. They represent the two possibilities to which the loading factors of the study participants can be likened the most, and therefore constitute the two dominating discourses on the subject matter at hand. The subject factor loadings of the study participants represent the factor loadings of each diplomat in this study in relation to the two idealized factors. Each of the two factors will be named in the following part of this section and a social perspective narrative will be created for it. It is important to note that this creation of a social perspective narrative arises out of the order of the statements given to them by the study participants, and therefore reflects the relative importance given to the statements in relation to each other. Furthermore, the results of the interview rounds with the diplomats are taken into account for the creation of the social perspective narratives as well.

Table 3
Statement Scores on Each Factor

No.		Factor	
		A	B
1	The United States is not open to an enlargement of the Security Council by a Charter amendment that changes the current veto structure.	1	4
2	Unlike Japan and Germany, which are most closely aligned with U.S. preferences, Brazil, India, and South Africa frequently vote contrary to U.S. preferences, showing that close bilateral relations do not always translate into cooperation in multilateral settings.	0	2
3	The United States supports expansion of the Security Council. Such expansion, however, should neither diminish the Council's effectiveness nor its efficiency.	1	2
4	The [German] Federal Government is also ready to shoulder the responsibility that comes along with a permanent membership on the security council.	3	-2
5	Every modification of the veto right will meet substantial resistance from the side of the five permanent members.	3	3
6	For Washington, an ideal enlargement scenario might be simply adding the G4 powers as permanent (or long-term) members without veto power.	-1	2
7	Given that U.S. interests in enlargement are riding on the future behavior of aspirant countries, the United States would do well to pursue a disciplined, criteria-based approach to enlargement.	2	0
8	Alongside the call for a geographically balanced distribution of seats, [...] countries that make considerable contributions to the UN should be members of the Security Council.	4	1
9	When the Security Council legislates, it sets rules for the United Nations membership as a whole.	1	-1
10	The UN may be a multilateral organisation, but it has to deal with an increasingly unipolar world in which the US rules, and rules supremely.	-3	-1
11	The United States is open in principle to a limited expansion of both permanent and non-permanent members.	0	1
12	The present institutional setting is able neither to appease existing conflicts nor to prevent those in preparation.	1	-1
13	The council's capability to act increases when preferably highly contributing states like Japan and Germany receive permanent seats on the council.	2	0
14	The heated debate in the general assembly has caused a sort of competition in multilateralism [...].	-2	1
15	The membership of the Security Council shall be increased from fifteen to twenty-five by adding six permanent and four non-permanent members.	0	-2

No.		Factor	
		A	B
16	The one who possesses considerable financial and other resources and puts them into the service of the UN, should also have the appropriate influence.	2	-1
17	There should be no changes to the current veto structure.	-4	3
18	The debate over the expansion of the Security Council is a geopolitical contest for power and influence, but it is also about sharing the cost of international security.	0	2
19	Germany has in all its decisions on the security council always taken into account EU interests […].	0	0
20	The major advantage of the G4 candidates' case rests on its trajectory towards a fairer representation of regional interests.	0	-1
21	40 years after the establishment of the United Nations, it is not only desirable today but entirely feasible to give serious thought to the reform of the United Nations and its system of organizations.	-1	1
22	This [institution of the veto] has merely widened the gap in the situation between the inhabitants of developed and developing countries dramatically: lack of security and war have been reserved for the most underprivileged peoples.	-1	-2
23	Vetoing U.N. action against a state that is clearly in violation of international law and practice because that state is an ally should not be acceptable.	2	-4
24	In order to keep the UN under its authority, the US is still in arrears for the payment of its contribution […].	-2	0
25	There is too much to lose if U.S. allows the enlargement debate to turn into a ruthless realpolitik chess game.	-3	0
26	[…] the idea of a possible enlargement of the Security Council progressed and received support from the US, in order to permit the entrance of Japan and Germany as permanent members.	-1	0
27	The global North […] finds itself in a permanent minority, outvoted on issue after issue by nations of the global South […].	-1	1
28	The word "permanent" does not belong in any constitution or charter, for the simple reason that no human creation is truly permanent.	-2	-3
29	It is hardly surprising […] that there is now wide sentiment that the time has come to enlarge the Council yet again, by anywhere from two to ten new members.	0	0
30	The reference to the status of Germany as the third largest contributor is a classical argument of Machtpolitik.	-2	0
31	Membership of the Security Council shall be increased from fifteen to twenty-four by adding five permanent and four non-permanent members.	1	-2
32	The four new non-permanent members of the Security Council shall be elected according to the following pattern: (i) One from African States; (ii) One from Asian States; (iii) One from Eastern European States; (iv) One from Latin American and Caribbean States.	0	-3
Own calculations.			

4.2.1. Convinced Institutionalism (Factor A)[25]

The most important aspect of United Nations Security Council membership is that it takes into account both geography and contributions. The UN Security Council should therefore be updated, based on a fair distribution of members. Such a distribution should take into account the geographical diversity of the membership, as well as the amount of contributions by United Nations member states (8). The legitimacy of the council depends on such a fair distribution, so that all members feel directly or indirectly represented and involved. Such contributions may be military, financial or diplomatic. Any reform must include a change to the current veto structure to include the newly selected permanent member states. Any reform without an expansion of veto powers would not be reflective of the 21st century (17). It is crucial that any permanent member state of the council has the capabilities to fulfill its role and is ready to shoulder the burden that comes with it. Germany would be one of those countries ready to do so, after having arisen from its past of a divided state during the years of the Cold War (4). It should be allowed to play its role for peace, security and stability in the world. Since the United Nations is a truly multilateral organization, all permanent members should be seen as equals, and no country should attempt to undermine this through playing anachronistic games of Machtpolitik (10). Since the institutional structures of the UN Security Council include veto rights for the current P-5 members however, it is unlikely that a reform will happen, as the current veto powers are not interested in any change (5). Even though geopolitical realities have changed drastically since the end of World War II and the fall of the Berlin Wall, the P-5 members fear a loss of power, and will therefore attempt to block any reform effort. Nevertheless, the P-5, and especially the United States would do well in working towards an honest reform to make the United Nations fit for the 21st century, since otherwise there is a real danger that the UN Security Council loses its legitimacy in the eyes of the world. There is simply too much to lose if the reform debate becomes a ruthless adaptation of Realpolitik (25). As the only remaining superpower, the United States would do well in us-

25 Numbers in brackets indicate the corresponding statements in table 3.

ing a criteria-based approach to evaluate which aspirant countries it wants to support. After all, the future behavior of new permanent members on the Security Council will have a huge effect on its future actions (7). In any potential reform scenario, it should be recognized that the council's capability to act increases when member states with high contributions are made permanent. This way, their willingness to further intensify their contributions is increased (13). Therefore, it would be beneficial for a future Security Council to make states like Germany and Japan permanent members. This is not only a question of effectiveness and efficiency, but also of justice. Higher-contributing members should simultaneously yield greater influence in the organization for which they pay a higher membership fee than others (16). The debate about reform has not evolved into a hypocritical competition of multilateralism, but is driven by an honest will for a just reform (14). Even though, the United States does not seem to be keen on reform, it recognizes the dedicated proposals of aspirant states and continues to support the United Nations as an institution (24). It is obvious that potential permanent seats for aspirant states should reflect their contributions, thereby entrusting them with its full privileges to recognize the work of the most influential and trustworthy countries (28). This has absolutely nothing to do with Machtpolitik, but much rather shows a willingness to shape the world in a peaceful and stable manner (30). In a future UN Security Council it should be prohibited to veto any action of the council that goes against a state in violation of international law, as peace and stability in the world can only be guaranteed on a legally binding international consensus (23).

4.2.2. Cautious Institutionalism (Factor B)[26]

Any change to the current veto structure of the United Nations Security Council would constitute a risky, if not dangerous, gamble with world peace and security. Therefore, the United States should not be open to any amendment to the UN Charter that would change the status-quo of the veto (1). The broad consensus among the P-5 members

26 Numbers in brackets indicate the corresponding statements in table 3.

of the council to prevent this from happening, shows that a change to the veto structure would be extremely risky. After all, those five states are still the guarantors of security and stability in the world (5). Permanent membership with a veto right in the UN Security Council should be see as a pillar of stability, counter-weighing the UN General Assembly (28). The legitimacy of the council arises out of its effectiveness to keep the world secure and stable, further supporting the current veto structure. Therefore, permanent membership with veto rights is an essential aspect of the Security Council. The veto powers of the Security Council should remain free in their use of the veto right, in accordance with the UN Charter. This may also include vetoing action against a state in violation of international regulations that have been signed by some, but not by all (23). Again, only what is specified in the UN Charter is legally binding. A change of the veto would most likely create more chaos and should not even be debated (17). As changes to the veto structure would surely include an expansion of veto rights to more countries, it is uncertain to what extent a future UN Security Council would still be able to act and to ensure peace. The United Nations voting record of other countries has shown that close bilateral ties do not always mean agreement in multilateral settings such as the Security Council. This can be backed up by the differing voting record of, for example, Germany and Japan on the one side, Brazil and India on the other side. While the first two can be seen as close U.S. allies, the latter two often align themselves with other blocs within the United Nations (2). Following this logic, one should attempt to get one's allies on board, while attempting to keep one's adversaries out. As no such one-sided reform effort would reach a majority in the United Nations General Assembly, no reform is preferable to bad reform. This applies to all P-5 powers alike. More member states on the council would make it more difficult to act. Therefore, an enlargement to both twenty-four or twenty-five members would be the absolute limit, if not already too much (15, 31). The various reform proposals over the last twenty years have only confused the UN membership, but have not improved the situation at all (32). The ideal enlargement would simply be adding the "G-4 powers". A really important criteria for Security Council membership is whether a country is ready and willing to fulfill its role. Emerging, powerful aspirant countries like Germany do not yet seem ready to do so, as it lacks crucial military capacities to deploy its forces at any time around the world to respond to threats against international peace and security (4). Furthermore, it is extremely important to keep the Security Council's ability to act in place. A too great expansion with too many differing interests would further undermine the council's effectiveness and efficiency in an already difficult setting (3). Again, the perfect solution would be to add the so-called "G-4 powers" of Brazil, Germany, India and Japan to only have emerging powerful countries on board. This would increase the council's capabilities due to those states' resources and contributions to the United Nations. At the same time this would reflect a good geographical distribution, balancing out differing interests on the council (6). While it would be really lamentable to ignore Africa in this, there does not seem to be a single country on the African continent capable of doing the same job as the "G-4 powers" would be capable of doing. It is obvious that, due to the importance of the UN Security Council, the reform debate is a geopolitical contest for power and influence. At the same time however, it is a question of justly sharing the cost for international security among the countries of the world (18). The institution of the veto does not constitute a dividing factor among different regional, geographical or political blocs within the United Nations, but ensures stability in the United Nations and the world from which all countries benefit (22).

4.2.3. Diplomats' Alignment to the two Discourses (Factor Loadings)

The factor loadings analysis of this thesis describes the individual factor loadings of the ten diplomats being studied [see table 4]. The loadings show how each of the diplomats correlates with the two factors found. One especially noteworthy factor between the ten diplomats that participated in this study is that the Germans and Americans overwhelmingly sided with opposing factors. Four out of the five German diplomats had a high positive correlation with Convinced Institutionalism. All of them had worked for their country in relations with the United Nations. Three out of five Americans had a high positive correlation with Cautious Institutionalism. Two from those had worked for their country in relations with the United Nations, while one had not. One German diplomat did not have a statistically significant correlation with Convinced Institutionalism, but solely a high negative correlation with Cautious Institutionalism. This diplomat had not worked in relations with the United Nations. One American diplomat did not have a statistically significant correlation with Cautious Institutionalism, but a high positive correlation with Convinced Institutionalism. This diplomat had also not worked in relations with the United Nations. Another American diplomat, who had not worked in relations with the United Nations, did not have statistically significant correlations with either one of the two factors. Thus, an overall of five [four Germans; one American] diplomats fell on factor A, while three [all Americans] fell on factor B. One German diplomat only showed statistical significance in his opposition to factor B. Following this, German diplomats showed greater consistency in their preference for factor A than American diplomats showed for factor B. Another interesting result is that on both sides, female diplomats were congruent with their national peers' dominating preference, while some male diplomats varied from it.

Table 4
Subjects Factor Loadings

			Factor	
Subjects			**A**	**B**
1	Diplomat (UN experience)	GER - (female)	0.66 *	-0.06
2	Diplomat (UN experience)	GER - (male)	0.76 *	-0.03
3	Diplomat (UN experience)	GER - (female)	0.72 *	-0.19
4	Diplomat (UN experience)	GER - (male)	0.61 *	0.14
5	Diplomat (no UN experience)	GER - (male)	0.40	-0.77 *
6	Diplomat (no UN experience)	USA - (female)	-0.01	0.32
7	Diplomat (UN experience)	USA - (male)	0.38	0.68 *
8	Diplomat (UN experience)	USA - (male)	-0.33	0.53 *
9	Diplomat (no UN experience)	USA - (male)	0.39	0.73 *
10	Diplomat (no UN experience)	USA - (male)	0.70 *	0.07
*p <_ 0.01. – Own calculations.				

A statistical factor correlations analysis was attempted with three rotating factors, but did not show sufficient statistical significance to justify the creation of a third factor. In this potential third factor, all German diplomats and three American diplomats did not have any correlation with the potential third discourse, while two Americans diplomats had a high positive and high negative correlation respectively.

4.3. Assessment of Typologies

The creation of the two social perspective narratives under consideration of the factor analysis and the interviews has given way to two different discourse typologies in a cross-national comparison of German and American diplomats: 1. Convinced Institutionalism & 2. Cautious Institutionalism [see table 5].

Table 5
Analysis of Two Discourses of UN Security Council Reform

	Discourse Elements			
Discourse	***Ontology***	***Agency***	***Ascribed Motivation***	***Relationships seen as natural***
Convinced Institutionalism	UN Member States, UN Security Council	Governments, UN Secretariat	Fair Distribution, Legitimacy	Capability to Contribute
Cautious Institutionalism	UN Member States, UN Security Council	Governments, UN Secretariat	Security & Stability, Effectiveness & Efficiency, Legitimacy	Capability to Act

Both of these discourses are similar to each other in some aspects and differ from each other in others. The similarities between them lie in their assessments of ontology and agency. Both discourses agree that the entities involved in the issue at hand are the UN member states and the UN Security Council. It is precisely the UN Security Council whose reform is at stake, and this organ is similarly recognized as the most important decision-making institution in this process. The second entity recognized is the member states of the United Nations which will ultimately have to decide upon any reform solution. Furthermore, the two discourses are in agreement over the agencies involved in the reform process, identifying them as national governments and the UN Secretariat. Thus, reform negotiations are an interplay between the involved member states' governments, and the United Nations as an institution. Differences can be identified in the ascribed motivations of the two discourses. Convinced Institutionalism acts on the motivations of reaching a fair distribution of member states on the Security Council, based on geographical diversity and contribution size to the UN. In addition, legitimacy is seen as arising out of exactly this fair distribution. Contributing countries should have proportional power in the UN system. The status-quo of the Security Council set-up is thus identified as lacking legitimacy. Cautious Institutionalism on the other side acts on the motivations of seeking security and stability for the world, seeing this best guaranteed with a continued status-quo of the remaining big military powers. Furthermore, effectiveness and efficiency serve as another motivation for this discourse, as the council should be kept capable to act swift and decisively. Any enlargement would complicate this heavily. Legitimacy is seen as arising out of the effectiveness and efficiency of the council, as well as out of a legally positivistic view of the status of the UN Charter being as it is. The relationship seen as natural constitutes a hierarchy that is assumed by the two discourses. While Convinced Institutionalism sees that hierarchy as being the capability of a UN member state to contribute to the institution, Cautious Institutionalism sees it as the capability of a member state to act in lieu of the institution. When looking at the factors loadings [see table 4], it is especially striking that almost all German and American diplomats sided with opposing factors. Only one German and one American diplomat differed from their peers, with the German diplomat having no correlation on factor A (& a negative correlation on factor B) and the American diplomat having a positive correlation on factor A (& no correlation on factor B). A reason for this divergence might be a difference in past experience throughout the diplomatic career. While all diplomats from both sides who had worked in relations with the United Nations stuck with their peers, the two diplomats that did not, had no past posting to the United Nations. Other diplomats without past posting to the United Nations however, did not differ from their peers. Overall, the German diplomats are slightly more consistent than the American diplomats on their respective factor.

Broadly speaking, the two discourses identified in this study can be accredited to two theories of international relations. While Convinced Institutionalism fits into the realm of liberal institutionalism, Cautious Institutionalism fits into the realm of liberal realism. Convinced Institutionalism reflects a conviction of the sanctity of international organizations such as the United Nations. It sees benefits in cooperation through the UN framework and in the building of a legally binding, international behavioral rulebook. This must be established through the incorporation of all member states on just terms, resembling the current situation within the international system. It is important to note that there is no idealistic dream driving this, but the rational assessment of the anarchic system being tameable through international institutions to create prosperity and peace. Broadly speaking, Convinced Institutionalism therefore can be related to the international relations theory of liberalism as outlined by prominent scholars and thinkers Adam Smith (1776), Immanuel Kant (1795), Michael Doyle (1983; 1986) John Ikenberry (2001) and Robert Keohane (1984; 1993). Liberalism holds that with growing international exchange, interdependence and laws, armed conflict between states can be reduced. Cautious Institutionalism reflects a more hesitant approach towards international organizations, for this study, specifically the United Nations. While it sees benefits in cooperating on the UN Security Council and shaping the world through common, international agreements, it simultaneously holds deep mistrust for the actions of other member states. It recognizes that within the UN system, some members states are more equal than others, and thus, preparations have to be taken. A state should therefore only cooperate within a UN framework as far as it is in its own rational interests, but always be ready to act outside of it where ever seen necessary. This discourse broadly can be related to the theoretical school of realism in international relations as outlined by prominent scholars Hans Morgenthau (1948), Kenneth Waltz (1959),

John Mearsheimer (1983; 2001), Stephen Walt (1987) or Robert Gilpin (1981; 1987). More precisely however, Cautious Institutionalism fits into the English school of the so-called liberal realism, as outlined by scholars Hedley Bull (1977; 1984), Martin Wight (1977; 1996; 2002) or Barry Buzan (2014). Liberal Realism assumes the international system to be anarchic, just as classical realism does. However, instead of pitting states against one another in an ever-constant struggle for power and a continuing mistrust of the others' intentions, liberal realism assumes there to be a society of states notwithstanding the omnipresent anarchy. This society of states arises out of the existence of common interests and norms between certain states, thus leading to the formulation of common rules of procedure when dealing with each other. The United Nations can be seen as the product of those common interests and norms, whose authority nevertheless solely reaches to said communalities. Both Convinced Institutionalism and Cautious Institutionalism can thus be broadly related to already existing theories within international politics. It is important to note that both theories assume rational actor behavior and stem from functionalistic goals. Both agree on the merit of the existence of international institutions, but disagree on the scope one's own interests should be put behind the institution's goals.

Following the development of the two theories of international politics, one can say that the Grotian English School of realism is already a middle ground between the Hobbesian classical realism and the Kantian liberal institutionalism. The Hobbesian classical liberalism sees states pitted against each other in a constant struggle for power and domination. The Kantian liberal institutionalism envisions a cosmopolitan society in which states cooperate through international institutions. The Grotian tradition of the English School accepts states as the principal actor in the system, but does not necessarily see everything as a zero-sum game. While the political discourse found for the United States falls in the Grotian tradition, the political discourse found for Germany falls in the Kantian tradition. Similar to the verbal battle between realism and liberalism in academia, one can expect that no immediate bridge will be found between the two identified political discourses either. Germany and the United States seem to be victims of the UN Security Council's structure, victims of the rules of the game.

After the interviews held with the four diplomats, it appears that the goal of their countries' actions is the accumulation of greater power in relation to others by introducing the arguments of distribution/legitimacy and security/stability respectively, thereby behaving as a rational actor in game theory. It is to be doubted that in switched situations, the two countries would act fundamentally differently than what game theory suggests. Therefore, domestic politics, historical backgrounds, cultural prevelance, etc. do not seem to have a great influence in institutionalized negotiation situations like the one at hand.

5. Limitations

As any scientific study, this master thesis has limitations to the method and scope. As mentioned in the methodology section of this study, Q-Methodology is not designed for representativeness of the sample size, but merely seeks to analyze a small number of policy experts. The minimal floor of ten participants in this study constitutes a very small sample size which was caused by the inaccessibility of more diplomats. Gaining access to a rather taciturn profession proved to be difficult for a student at the graduate level. Therefore, it might be interesting to see the results of a study with more participants from either the diplomatic services or the general public. It further remains speculative whether a greater sample size would have allowed the creation of another discourse to give way to a compromise.

6. Conclusion

After having illustrated a historical development of the debate on UN Security Council reform from the early 1990s until today, and further having analyzed the results from the factor correlations and Q-Analysis on attitudes of German and American diplomats regarding said reform, two cross-national discourses could be identified. Judging from the elements of discourse, the two discourses are extremely similar in their considerations of ontology and agency, while their motivations and assumptions of natural relationships differ sharply. The discourses show two opposing argumentative strains on the issue with one concentrating on justice in the distribution and justice in the representativeness concerning contributions [Convinced Institutionalism], the other concentrating on world security and council effectiveness [Cautious Institutionalism]. The alignment of German and American diplomats has shown a fault line between the countries' positions, with Germans predominantly siding with the first and Americans predominantly siding with the latter. Thus, with the methodological approach used in this thesis, no compromising discourse could be identified and no immediate solution appears, allowing the status-quo of policy positions to prevail. For the case between Germany and the United States, Q-Methodology was able to clearly mirror the rift on policy positions on UN Security Council reform through factor analysis. It seems that there is no new way forward, as the UN Security Council seems to be a victim of its structural set-up.

Q-Methodology was able to clearly identify the current deadlock on UN Security Council reform between Germany and the United States. The deadlock consists of the United States not wanting to change the current veto structure. Germany on the other side, feels that it deserves to be rewarded with a veto upgrade in its international standing in the United Nations. While the two countries do not seem to be that far away from each other generally, their two positions remain directly opposed to each other on this singular issue. One possible solution might be Germany accepting a permanent seat on the council without a veto right. Even after the proposed reform by the Group of Four, including a 15-year review period, no veto right should be granted. However, Germany would most likely not be interested in such a solution due to an increasing homogeneity in the EU-member states' foreign policy goals. With an increased importance in the world, Germany expects to be voted to the UN Security Council as a non-permanent member regularly in the future. Due to the expected future homogeneity in EU-member states' foreign policy goals, a permanent seat without a veto right for Germany would thus not be a recognizable upgrade for the country.

In spite of the current deadlock, during further negotiations on UN Security Council reform, Germany and the United States might want to take into account a combination of the proposal by the Group of Four, the factor "time" as mentioned in Alexopoulos et al. (2007), and the "long-term approach" as mentioned in McDonald and Stewart (2010). The reform proposal of the Group of Four calls for expanding permanent membership without the veto power during the first 15 years, but includes a review afterwards on the potential of granting the veto power. This would lastingly establish a permanent status, but without the veto right for the first 15 years. In accordance with articles 108 and 109 of the United Nations Charter, the review after the 15 years would have to culminate in a final decision by the UN General Assembly on the granting of the veto right to the new permanent members. Instead of proposing charter amendments to this regard, the time until a review should be extended to 30 years to match the changes of the unanimity core as outlined by Alexopoulos et al. (2007). He predicts the P-5 countries' voting behavior on the UN Security Council to become more similar with China's and Russia's transition to the industrialized world, thus making P-5 agreement on future permanent membership candidates with veto powers more likely. Furthermore, Germany and the United States should seek a recommendation of the Security Council itself prior to the General Assembly review, giving P-5 and aspirant countries the chance for deliberation. The long-term approach as outlined in McDonald and Stewart (2010), would allow aspirant countries to prove their willingness and capability to shoulder the burden of permanent membership during the 30 years. This would create a status of preliminary permanent membership without veto right. At the end of the 30-year period would then stand the option of upgrade to the veto right or the option of downgrade back to non-permanent membership, depending on the result of the deliberation between P-5 and aspirant countries. The two categories of countries would have the chance to come to an agreement on the aspirant countries' performance. After already having allowed a 30-year period of preliminary permanent membership for the aspirant countries, pressure on the P-5 would be increased, making a rejection less likely. Yet simultaneously, the P-5 could reserve their right of exclusivity over the reform before any review by the UN General Assembly should they deem UN Security Council stability in danger by a permanent reform.

Taking Q-Methodology further, as more countries will eventually have to be involved in the reform process, it might be interesting to undertake more Q-methodological studies comparing other countries on the same issue. Since there are so many different reform proposals by different groups or panels, Q-Methodology could serve as a structuring tool for finding common patterns among them. Further interesting Q-methodological studies in this direction could be a comparison of Germany with France and Italy respectively. These comparisons would enable us to look for common ground between the most promising aspirant country and its closest ally among the P-5 countries. Furthermore, a comparison with Italy could look for common ground between the two rivaling proposals of the Group of Four and Uniting for Consensus.

A comparison of this thesis' two countries has not shown a clear path forward in terms of a joint policy. As can be found in Hosli et al. (2011), the veto powers on the UN Security Council are the only members with a decisive weighted voting share. Therefore, a five-way comparison of the P-5 countries could be another promising Q-methodological study. Such a study could show the common ground on operational reform proposals. This suggestion is also to be looked at in relation to George Tsebelis' (2002) veto player theory. Especially the unanimity core within that theory seems interesting, as a Q-methodological study among all P-5 could also showcase such a core. While he argues that all policy proposals within the unanimity core uphold the status-quo, Alexopoulos, et al. (2007) have shown that another factor being added to the calculation could bring change. With changing policy preferences over time, the unanimity core of the council changes as well. Should a Q-methodological study among the P-5 countries show different political discourses, a change of the unanimity core could be verified. Repetitive studies of the P-5 countries over time would enable us to track the movement of the unanimity core.

References

African Union. (2005). The Common African Position On The Proposed Reform Of The United Nations – "The Ezulwini Consensus". (March 8th, 2005). http://www.un.org/en/africa/osaa/pdf/au/cap_screform_2005.pdf.

African Union. (2005). Sirte Declaration On The Reform Of The United Nations. (July 5th, 2005). Assembly/AU/Decl. 2 (V). http://www.au.int/en/sites/default/files/decisions/9552-assembly_en_4_5_july_2005_auc_fifth_ordinary_session_decisions_declarations_and_resolution.pdf.

Alexopoulos, A. & Bourantonis, D. (2007). The Reform of the UN Security Council: A Veto-Player Analysis. Department of Political Science, University of Crete.

Alker, H. R., Jr. & Sylvan, D. (1986). Political Discourse Analysis. Presented at the annual meeting of the American Political Science Association, Washington.

Ariyoruk, A. (2005). Players and Proposals in the Security Council Debate. Global Policy Forum. https://www.globalpolicy.org/component/content/article/200/41204.html.

Asthana, A. & Grierson, J. (2016, May 10th). Afghanistan and Nigeria 'possibly most corrupt countries', Cameron lets slip. The Guardian. https://www.theguardian .com/uk-news/2016/may/10/david-cameron-afghanistan-nigeria-possibly-most-corrupt-countries.

Auswärtiges Amt. (2014). Bericht der Bundesregierung zur Zusammenarbeit zwischen der Bundesrepublik Deutschland und den Vereinten Nationen und einzelnen, globalagierenden, internationalen Organisationen und Institutionen im Rahmen des VN-Systems in den Jahren 2012 und 2013. (September 3rd, 2014).

Auswärtiges Amt. (2016). Deutsche Kandidatur für den Sicherheitsrat 2019/2020. http://www.auswaertiges-amt.de/nn_582140/sid_1D24DC9675AA84A941A88CC236A8F6FF/DE/Aussenpolitik/Friedenspolitik/VereinteNationen/07_Sicherheitsrat/Sicherheitsrat.html?nnm=582138.

Auswärtiges Amt. (2016). Reform des Sicherheitsrats der Vereinten Nationen. http://www.auswaertiges-amt.de/DE/Aussenpolitik/Friedenspolitik/ Vereinte-Nationen/5_Reformen/ReformSR_node.html.

Baas, L. R. (1997). The interpersonal sources of the development of political images: An intensive, longitudinal study. Operant Subjectivity, Vol. 20, pp. 117–142.

Bertrand, M. (1985). Some Reflections of Reform of the United Nations. United Nations Joint Inspection Unit. Geneva: United Nations.

Bosco, D. (2015). The United States Doesn't Want To Reform The UN Security Council. Foreign Policy. http://foreignpolicy.com/2015/09/29/the-united-states-doesnt-want-to-reform-the-u-n-security-council/ .

Brown, S. R. (1980). Political subjectivity: Applications of Q methodology in political science. New Haven, CT: Yale University Press.

Bull, H. (1977). The Anarchical Society – A Study of Order in World Politics. Columbia University Press: New York, NY.

Bull, H. (1984). The Expansion of International Society. Oxford University Press.

Bundesregierung. (2015). Joint Press Statement at the Meeting of Leaders of the G-4 countries- Brazil, Germany, India and Japan – on United Nations Security Council Reform. https://www.bundesregierung.de/Content/EN/ Pressemitteilungen/BPA/2015/2015-09-29-g4-sicherheitsrat_en.html.

Butler, R. (2012). Reform of the United Nations Security Council. Penn State Journal of Law & International Affairs. Vol. 1 (1), 23–39.

Buzan, B. (2014). An Introduction to the English School of International Relations: The Societal Approach. Cambridge, Polity.

Byung, S. L. & Wonhi, S. (2001). Investor response to online stock trading: A study using Q methodology. Operant Subjectivity, Vol. 24, pp. 109–131.

Carlson, J. M. & Trichtinger, R. (2001). Perspectives on entertainment television's portrayal of a racial incident: An intensive analysis. Communication Review, Vol. 4, pp. 253–278.

Charter of the United Nations. (1946). Chapter V, Article 24, Paragraph 1.

Charter of the United Nations. (1946). Chapter V, Article 24, Paragraph 2.

Charter of the United Nations. (1946). Chapter V, Article 25.

Charter of the United Nations. (1946). Chapter VI.

Charter of the United Nations. (1946). Chapter VII.

Charter of the United Nations. (1946). Chapter VIII.

Charter of the United Nations. (1946). Chapter VIII, Article 53.

Charter of the United Nations. (1946). Chapter XII.

Charter of the United Nations. (1946). Chapter XII, Article 77.

Charter of the United Nations. (1946). Chapter XVII, Article 107.

Chen, A. (1996). Student interest in activities in a second physical education curriculum: An analysis in student subjectivity. Research Quarterly for Exercise and Sport, Vol. 67, pp. 424–432.

Council on Foreign Relations. (2015). The Role of the General Assembly. http://www.cfr.org/international-organizations-and-alliances/role-un-general-assembly/p13490.

Das Bundesarchiv. Die Hallstein-Doktrin. (1955). https://www.bundesarchiv.de/oeffentlichkeitsarbeit/bilder_dokumente/01366/index-2.html.de .

Deutsche Gesellschaft für die Vereinten Nationen. (2016). 40 Years of German Membership in the United Nations. http://www.dgvn.de/germany-in-the-united-nations/40-years-of-german-membership-in-the-united-nations/.

Doyle, M. (1983). Kant, Liberal Legacies, and Foreign Affairs. Phylosophy and Public Affairs, Vol. 12 (3), pp. 205–235.

Doyle, M. (1986). Liberalism and World Politics. The American Political Science Review, Vol. 80 (4), pp. 1151–1169.

Dryzek, J. S. & Berejikian, J. (1993). Reconstructive Democratic Theory. The American Political Science Review, Vol. 87 (1), pp. 48–60.

Dryzek, J. S. & Braithwaite, V. (2000). On the prospects for democratic deliberation: Values analysis applied to Australian politics. Political Psychology, Vol. 21, pp. 241–266.

Febbraro, A. R. (1995). On the epistemology, metatheory, and ideology of Q methodology: A critical analysis. In Ian Lubek, Rene Van Hezewijk, Gail Pheterson & Charles. W. Tolman, Trends and issues in theoretical psychology (pp.144–150). New York: Springer.

Fischer, J. (2004). Speech before the German Bundestag http://dip.bundestag.de/btp/15/15122.pdf. (September 8th, 2004).

Gallivan, J. (1994). Subjectivity and the psychology of gender: Q as a feminist methodology. In Joanne Gallivan, Sharon D. Crozier & Vivian M. Lalande, Women, girls, and achievement (pp. 29–36). Toronto: Captus University Publications.

Genscher, H. D. (1990). Speech by Foreign Minister Genscher at the 45th United Nations General Assembly in New York. Bulletin 115/1990: 1201–1206. (September 26th, 1990).

Gowan, R. (2013). Germany and the Security Council: Neither too strong nor too weak. VereinteNationen: German Review on the United Nations, Vol. 61 (1), pp. 3–8.

Gilpin, R. (1981). War and Change In World Politics. Cambridge University Press: UK.

Gilpin, R. (1987). Princeton University Press: Princeton, NJ.

Hellmann, G. & Roos, U. (2007). Das deutsche Streben nach einem ständigen Sitz im UN-Sicherheitsrat – Analyse eines Irrwegs und Skizzen eines Auswegs. Institut für Entwicklung und Frieden. Universität Duisburg-Essen. INEF-Report 92/2007.

Hosli, M. O.; Moody, R.; O'Donovan, B.; Kaniovski, S. & Little, A. C. H. (2011). Squaring the Circle? Collective and distributive effects of United Nations Security Council reform. The Review of International Organizations, Vol. 6, pp. 163–187.

Intergovernmental Negotiations. Framework Document – As populated by states. (May 4th, 2015). http://centerforunreform.org/sites/default/files/050515_security-council-reform-framework-document.pdf#overlay-context= .

International Monetary Fund. World Economic Outlook Database. (July, 2016).

Ikenberry, J. (2001). After Victory: Institutions, Strategic Restraint, and the Rebuilding of Order after Major Wars. Princeton University Press: Princeton, NJ.

Kant, I. (1795). Zum ewigen Frieden – Ein philosophischer Entwurf.

Keohane, R. (1984). After Hegemony: Power and Discord in the World Political Economy. Princeton University Press, Princeton NJ.

Keohane, R. (1993). Institutional Theory and the Realist Challenge after the Cold War. In "Neorealism and Neoliberalism: The Contemporary Debate. Columbia University Press: New York. NY.

Kogan, S. M.; Walters, L. H. & Daniels, T. (2002). Contextual assessment of couples therapy: the clinical discourse Q-set. Journal of Marital & Family Therapy, Vol. 28 (4), pp. 409–422.

Lecouteur, A. & Delfabbro, P. H. (2001). Repertoires of teaching and learning: A comparison of university teachers and students using Q methodology. Higher Education, Vol. 42, pp. 205–235.

Lyman, P. N. (2000). Saving the UN Security Council – A Challenge for the United States. Max Planck Yearbook of the United Nations. Vol. 4, 127–146.

McDonald, K.C. & Patrick, S. M. (2010). Security Council Enlargement and U.S. Interests. Council on Foreign Relations. Special Report No. 59.

Mearsheimer, J. (1983). Conventional Deterrence. Cornell University Press: Ithaca, NY.

Mearsheimer, J. (2001). The Tragedy of Great Power Politics. W. W. Norton & Company: New York, NY.

Meisler, S. (1995). United Nations: The First Fifty Years. Atlantic Monthly Press. New York, NY.

Morgenthau, H. (1948). Politics Among Nations. Knopf: New York, NY.

Mosyagina, N. I.; Kashin, A. B. & Peck, R. L. (1997). Emerging Russian consumerism. A Q-Methodology study of consumer attitudes after Perestroika. Congress Manuscipt. Presented at the "Annual Conference on the Scientific Study of Subjectivity". Syracuse, New York.

Müller, F. H. & Kals, E. (2004). Die Q-Methode. Ein innovatives Verfahren zur Erhebung subjektiver Einstellungen und Meinungen. Forum: Qualitative Sozialforschung, Vol. 5 (2), Art. 34.

Plett, B. (2012). Small countries call for more transparency at the United Nations. BBC News. http://www.bbc.com/news/world-us-canada-18123768.

Pleuger, G. (2003). Die Reform des Sicherheitsrates der Vereinten Nationen. In Sabine von Schorlemer. Praxishandbuch UNO – Die Vereinten Nationen im Lichte globaler Herausforderungen, Heidelberg.

Richard, R. (2000). A methodological approach to national identity in Europe. Politique Européenne, Vol. 1, pp. 84–107.

Schwartzberg, J. E. (2005). Getting it wrong on Security Council Reform. Institute for Global Policy, World Federalist Movement.

Schwartzberg, J. E. (2004). Revitalizing the United Nations – Reform through weighted voting. Institute for Global Policy, World Federalist Movement.

Schwartzberg, J. E. (2007). Small States and UN Reform. Institute for Global Policy, World Federalist Movement.

Schwartzberg, J. E. (2013). Transforming the United Nations System: Designs for a Workable World. United Nations University Press.

Schweizerische Eidgenossenschaft. (2009). Intergovernmental Negotiations on the Reform of the Security Council, Debate on Working Methods, Informal Plenary. Permanent Mission of Switzerland to the United Nations, New York, NY.

Seidel, G. (1985). Political Discourse Analysis. In Handbook of Discourse Analysis ed. Teun A. van Dijk. London: Academic.

Shepsle, K. A. (2005). "Rational Choice Institutionalism". Harvard University.

Shilin, M.; Khaimina, O.; Kluikov, Y. & Lukyanov, S. (2000). Coping strategies: The white sea case (Northern Russia). http://www.uit.no/MostCCPP/Huhmari/joe_pap/JOE_Michael-S.pdf .

Singer, J. B. (1997). Chances and consistencies: Newspaper journalists contemplate an online uture. Newspaper Research Journal, Vol. 18, pp. 2–18.

Singer, J. B.; Craig, D.; Allen, C. W.; Whitehouese, V., Dimitrova, A. & Sanders, K. P. (1996). Attitudes of professors and students about new media technology. Journalism and Mass Communication Educator, Vol. 51 (2), pp. 36–45.

Smith, A. (1776). An Inquiry into the Nature and Causes of the Wealth of Nations. London: W. Strahan.

Stephenson, W. (1935). Correlation persons instead of tests. Character and Personality, 4, 17–24.

Stephenson, W. (1953). The study of behavior: Q-technique and its methodology. Chicago: University of Chicago Press.

The Economist. (2016). Brazil's Fall. http://www.economist.com/news/leaders/21684779-disaster-looms-latin-americas-biggest-economy-brazils-fall .

Thomas, D. B. & Baas, L. R. (1996). The postelection campaign: Competing constructions of the Clinton victory in 1992. The Journal of Politics, Vol. 58, pp. 309–331.

The White House. National Security Strategy. (May, 2010).

Toulmin, S. (1958). The Uses of Argument. Cambridge: Cambridge University Press.

Tsebelis, G. (2002). Veto Players: How Political Institutions Work. Princeton, NJ: Princeton University Press.

Ullmann, J. E. (1990). Who Won Cold War? Japanese and Germans. The New York Times. http://www.nytimes.com/1990/07/03/opinion/l-who-won-cold-war-japanese-and-germans-664690.html .

UN Summit Agenda. (2000, September 7th). BBC News. http://news.bbc.co.uk/2/hi/904903.stm .

United Nations. General Assembly Decision 62/557. Question of equitable representation on and increase in the membership of the Security Council and related matters. (September 15th, 2008).

United Nations. General Assembly Draft Resolution A/59/L.64. Security Council Reform. (July 6th, 2005).

United Nations. General Assembly Draft Resolution A/59/L.67. Question of equitable representation on and increase in the membership of the Security Council and related matters. (July 18h, 2005).

United Nations. General Assembly Draft Resolution A/59/L.68. Reform of the Security Council. (July 21st, 2005).

United Nations. General Assembly Draft Resolution A/60/L.49. Improving the working methods of the Security Council. (March 17th, 2006).

United Nations. General Assembly Presidential Note A/59/565. Follow-up to the outcome of the Millennium Summit. (December 2nd, 2004).

United Nations. General Assembly Resolution A/RES/47/62. Question of equitable representation on and increase in the membership of the Security Council. (December 11th, 1992).

United Nations. General Assembly Resolution A/RES/48/26. Question of equitable representation on and increase in the membership of the Security Council. (December 3rd, 1993).

United Nations. High-level Panel on Threats, Challenges and Change. A more secure world: Our shared responsibility. (December 2nd, 2004). http://www.un .org/en/peacebuilding/pdf/historical/hlp_more_secure_world.pdf.

United Nations. Secretariat Assessment ST/ADM/SER.B/932. Assessment of Member States' advances to the Working Capital Fund for the biennium 2016–2017 and contributions to the United Nations regular budget for 2016. (December 28th, 2015).

United Nations. Security Council Presidential Note S/2006/507. Note by the President of the Security Council. (July 19th, 2006).

United Nations. Security Council Resolution S/RES/687. (April 8th, 1991).

United Nations. Security Council Resolution S/RES/688. (April 5th, 1991).

United Nations. United Nations Millennium Declaration A/55/L.2. (December 14th, 2000).

United States Congress. 2005 United Nations Reform Act H.R.2745. (June 17th, 2005).

United States Department of State. (1999). Reform of the UN System.

United States Department of State. (2003). Reform of the UN System.

United States Department of State. (2004). Reform of the UN System.

United States Institute of Peace. (2006). American Interests and UN Reform – Report of the Task Force on the United Nations.

Uniting for Consensus Group. (2009). Security Council Reform. Global Policy Forum. https://www.globalpolicy.org/images/pdfs/UFC_2009_Proposal.pdf.

Walt, S. (1987). The Origins of Alliances. Cornell University Press: Ithaca, NY.

Waltz, K. (1959). Man, the State, and War. Columbia University Press: New York, NY.

Webler, T.; Danielson, S. & Tuler, S. (2009). Using Q Method to Reveal Social Perspectives in Environmental Research. Social and Environmental Research Institute. Greenfield, MA.

Wight, M. (1977). Systems of States. Leicester University Press, UK.

Wight, M. (1996). International Theory: The three Traditions. Leicester University Press, UK.

Wight, M. (2002). Power Politics. Bloomsbury Academic.

Winter, E. (1996). Voting and Vetoing. The American Political Science Review, Vol. 90 (4), pp. 813–823.

Wirkola, E. R. H. (2010). Reform of the UN Security Council and Veto Player Theory. University of Oslo.

Appendix

PQMethod2.35 UNSC Reform - Germany/United States PAGE 1
Path and Project Name: C:\PQMethod\projects/UNSCRE Jul 12 16

Correlation Matrix Between Sorts

SORTS	1	2	3	4	5	6	7	8	9	10
1 Diplomat	100	42	52	55	25	-6	11	1	14	12
2 Diplomat	42	100	50	28	25	9	20	-25	24	49
3 Diplomat	52	50	100	24	39	-10	10	-11	15	37
4 Diplomat	55	28	24	100	10	8	18	-8	25	33
5 Diplomat	25	25	39	10	100	-34	-23	-46	-32	19
6 Diplomat	-6	9	-10	8	-34	100	0	-5	8	8
7 Diplomat	11	20	10	18	-23	0	100	16	59	35
8 Diplomat	1	-25	-11	-8	-46	-5	16	100	15	-38
9 Diplomat	14	24	15	25	-32	8	59	15	100	28
10 Diplomat	12	49	37	33	19	8	35	-38	28	100

Unrotated Factor Matrix

	Factors							
	1	2	3	4	5	6	7	8
SORTS								
1 Diplomat	0.6618	-0.0610	0.5329	0.3449	-0.0325	-0.1475	0.0031	0.1666
2 Diplomat	0.7625	-0.0321	-0.1398	0.0540	0.3574	-0.2223	0.4407	-0.0956
3 Diplomat	0.7217	-0.1937	0.2400	-0.0506	0.4339	0.1986	-0.3325	-0.0577
4 Diplomat	0.6142	0.1362	0.1792	0.4074	-0.5725	0.1219	0.0343	-0.1251
5 Diplomat	0.3900	-0.7766	0.0584	-0.2049	-0.0773	-0.0111	-0.0806	0.2077
6 Diplomat	-0.0095	0.3157	-0.5220	0.7015	0.2307	0.0538	-0.1392	0.2043
7 Diplomat	0.3815	0.6812	-0.0292	-0.4007	-0.0960	0.0405	0.0623	0.4475
8 Diplomat	-0.3238	0.5288	0.6176	0.0369	0.2393	0.3022	0.1574	-0.0482
9 Diplomat	0.3985	0.7284	-0.0178	-0.2130	-0.0232	-0.3204	-0.2800	-0.2197
10 Diplomat	0.6963	0.0689	-0.4865	-0.2110	-0.0815	0.3789	0.0714	-0.1389
Eigenvalues	2.9638	2.0426	1.2884	1.0764	0.7777	0.4677	0.4440	0.4109
% expl.Var.	30	20	13	11	8	5	4	4

PQMethod2.35 UNSC Reform - Germany/United States PAGE 2
Path and Project Name: C:\PQMethod\projects/UNSCRE Jul 12 16

Cumulative Communalities Matrix

Factors 1 Thru ....

SORTS	1	2	3	4	5	6	7	8
1 Diplomat	0.4379	0.4416	0.7256	0.8446	0.8456	0.8674	0.8674	0.8951
2 Diplomat	0.5814	0.5824	0.6020	0.6049	0.7326	0.7820	0.9763	0.9854
3 Diplomat	0.5209	0.5584	0.6160	0.6186	0.8068	0.8462	0.9568	0.9601
4 Diplomat	0.3773	0.3958	0.4279	0.5939	0.9218	0.9366	0.9378	0.9534
5 Diplomat	0.1521	0.7553	0.7587	0.8007	0.8067	0.8068	0.8133	0.8564
6 Diplomat	0.0001	0.0997	0.3722	0.8643	0.9175	0.9204	0.9398	0.9815
7 Diplomat	0.1456	0.6096	0.6105	0.7710	0.7802	0.7819	0.7857	0.9860
8 Diplomat	0.1049	0.3845	0.7659	0.7673	0.8246	0.9159	0.9407	0.9430
9 Diplomat	0.1588	0.6893	0.6896	0.7350	0.7355	0.8382	0.9166	0.9649
10 Diplomat	0.4849	0.4896	0.7263	0.7709	0.7775	0.9211	0.9262	0.9455
cum% expl.Var.	30	50	63	74	81	86	91	95

Factor Matrix with an X Indicating a Defining Sort

Loadings

QSORT	1	2
1 Diplomat	0.6622X	-0.0562
2 Diplomat	0.7627X	-0.0265
3 Diplomat	0.7232X	-0.1884
4 Diplomat	0.6132X	0.1407
5 Diplomat	0.3957	-0.7738X
6 Diplomat	-0.0118	0.3156
7 Diplomat	0.3765	0.6840X
8 Diplomat	-0.3277	0.5264X
9 Diplomat	0.3931	0.7313X
10 Diplomat	0.6958X	0.0741
% expl.Var.	30	20

```
PQMethod2.35              UNSC Reform - Germany/United States                    PAGE    3
Path and Project Name: C:\PQMethod\projects/UNSCRE                               Jul 12 16

Free Distribution Data Results

 QSORT             MEAN     ST.DEV.

  1 Diplomat      0.000      1.884
  2 Diplomat      0.000      1.884
  3 Diplomat      0.000      1.884
  4 Diplomat      0.000      1.884
  5 Diplomat      0.000      1.884
  6 Diplomat      0.000      1.884
  7 Diplomat      0.000      1.884
  8 Diplomat      0.000      1.884
  9 Diplomat      0.000      1.884
 10 Diplomat      0.000      1.884
```

PQMethod2.35 UNSC Reform - Germany/United States PAGE 4
Path and Project Name: C:\PQMethod\projects/UNSCRE Jul 12 16

Factor Scores with Corresponding Ranks

No.	Statement	No.	Factor 1	Rank	Factor 2	Rank
1	US not open enlarge by CH amend changes veto	1	0.51	10	2.61	1
2	Unlike J/D BRIC vote contrary US showing bilat not coo	2	0.20	15	0.87	6
3	US supports expan without diminish effec or effiec	3	0.48	11	0.88	5
4	Germany ready to shoulder resps with UNSC membership	4	1.42	3	-0.94	29
5	Modification of veto meets resistance of P5	5	1.49	2	2.19	2
6	For US idea enlargement is G4	6	-0.53	23	1.40	4
7	US interests depend on behavior, criteria-based approa	7	0.96	6	-0.12	15
8	Alongside geographical distrib, contributions should m	8	1.71	1	0.23	10
9	When SC legislates, sets rules for all UN	9	0.47	12	-0.42	21
10	UN may be multilat but world ruled by US	10	-1.67	31	-0.69	25
11	US open in princip to limited enlargement of UNSC	11	0.02	17	0.79	8
12	Current SC setting unable to appease or prevent confli	12	0.67	9	-0.48	22
13	SC capability increase when members with contribu J/D	13	1.20	5	-0.39	20
14	Debate in UNGA caused competition for multilateralism	14	-1.19	26	0.52	9
15	Membership of UNSC increase from 15 to 25 6per/4nonper	15	0.46	13	-0.81	28
16	State who has ressources should have incfluence	16	1.26	4	-0.52	23
17	There should be no changes to veto	17	-1.86	32	1.47	3
18	UNSC debate is about geopolitics but also int sec	18	-0.03	18	0.83	7
19	Germany has always taken EU interest into account	19	0.46	14	-0.11	14
20	Major advan of G4 rest on fair geog rep	20	-0.04	19	-0.55	24
21	40 years after estab, reform is desirable	21	-0.27	21	0.17	11
22	veto has widenend gap between devel/non devel world	22	-0.94	25	-0.73	26
23	veto action against breach of in law not accept	23	0.94	7	-2.13	32
24	To keep UN under auth US is in arrears of payments	24	-1.24	27	-0.20	17
25	Too much to lose in UNSC reform to make it realpol	25	-1.44	30	-0.14	16
26	Idea of UNSC ref support from US to make J/D members	26	-0.65	24	-0.27	19
27	Global north is perm outvoted by South	27	-0.46	22	0.09	12
28	Permanent not belong into constit as noting permanent	28	-1.40	29	-1.34	31
29	Not surpirsing that UNSC reform is called for	29	-0.20	20	-0.07	13
30	Reference to Germany as contrib is Machtpolitik	30	-1.29	28	-0.24	18
31	UNSC membership from 15 to 24 by 5per/4nonper	31	0.74	8	-0.77	27
32	4 new nonper 1 Afr, 1 Asi, 1 Eas.Eu, 1 LatAm	32	0.19	16	-1.12	30

Correlations Between Factor Scores

	1	2
1	1.0000	-0.0088
2	-0.0088	1.0000

PQMethod2.35 UNSC Reform - Germany/United States PAGE 5
Path and Project Name: C:\PQMethod\projects/UNSCRE Jul 12 16

Factor Scores -- For Factor 1

No.	Statement	No.	Z-SCORES
8	Alongside geographical distrib, contributions should mem	8	1.706
5	Modification of veto meets resistance of P5	5	1.489
4	Germany ready to shoulder resps with UNSC membership	4	1.422
16	State who has ressources should have incfluence	16	1.262
13	SC capability increase when members with contribu J/D	13	1.204
7	US interests depend on behavior, criteria-based approach	7	0.957
23	veto action against breach of in law not accept	23	0.945
31	UNSC membership from 15 to 24 by 5per/4nonper	31	0.743
12	Current SC setting unable to appease or prevent conflict	12	0.667
1	US not open enlarge by CH amend changes veto	1	0.513
3	US supports expan without diminish effec or effiec	3	0.480
9	When SC legislates, sets rules for all UN	9	0.468
15	Membership of UNSC increase from 15 to 25 6per/4nonper	15	0.465
19	Germany has always taken EU interest into account	19	0.465
2	Unlike J/D BRIC vote contrary US showing bilat not coop	2	0.200
32	4 new nonper 1 Afr, 1 Asi, 1 Eas.Eu, 1 LatAm	32	0.193
11	US open in princip to limited enlargement of UNSC	11	0.015
18	UNSC debate is about geopolitics but also int sec	18	-0.027
20	Major advan of G4 rest on fair geog rep	20	-0.039
29	Not surpirsing that UNSC reform is called for	29	-0.196
21	40 years after estab, reform is desirable	21	-0.266
27	Global north is perm outvoted by South	27	-0.465
6	For US idea enlargement is G4	6	-0.532
26	Idea of UNSC ref support from US to make J/D members	26	-0.646
22	veto has widenend gap between devel/non devel world	22	-0.939
14	Debate in UNGA caused competition for multilateralism	14	-1.187
24	To keep UN under auth US is in arrears of payments	24	-1.241
30	Reference to Germany as contrib is Machtpolitik	30	-1.292
28	Permanent not belong into constit as noting permanent	28	-1.397
25	Too much to lose in UNSC reform to make it realpol	25	-1.436
10	UN may be multilat but world ruled by US	10	-1.669
17	There should be no changes to veto	17	-1.860

PQMethod2.35 UNSC Reform - Germany/United States PAGE 6
Path and Project Name: C:\PQMethod\projects/UNSCRE Jul 12 16

Factor Scores -- For Factor 2

No.	Statement	No.	Z-SCORES
1	US not open enlarge by CH amend changes veto	1	2.606
5	Modification of veto meets resistance of P5	5	2.189
17	There should be no changes to veto	17	1.475
6	For US idea enlargement is G4	6	1.400
3	US supports expan without diminish effec or effiec	3	0.877
2	Unlike J/D BRIC vote contrary US showing bilat not coop	2	0.871
18	UNSC debate is about geopolitics but also int sec	18	0.835
11	US open in princip to limited enlargement of UNSC	11	0.789
14	Debate in UNGA caused competition for multilateralism	14	0.516
8	Alongside geographical distrib, contributions should mem	8	0.226
21	40 years after estab, reform is desirable	21	0.168
27	Global north is perm outvoted by South	27	0.086
29	Not surpirsing that UNSC reform is called for	29	-0.075
19	Germany has always taken EU interest into account	19	-0.113
7	US interests depend on behavior, criteria-based approach	7	-0.118
25	Too much to lose in UNSC reform to make it realpol	25	-0.140
24	To keep UN under auth US is in arrears of payments	24	-0.201
30	Reference to Germany as contrib is Machtpolitik	30	-0.235
26	Idea of UNSC ref support from US to make J/D members	26	-0.265
13	SC capability increase when members with contribu J/D	13	-0.394
9	When SC legislates, sets rules for all UN	9	-0.420
12	Current SC setting unable to appease or prevent conflict	12	-0.480
16	State who has ressources should have incfluence	16	-0.516
20	Major advan of G4 rest on fair geog rep	20	-0.552
10	UN may be multilat but world ruled by US	10	-0.690
22	veto has widenend gap between devel/non devel world	22	-0.726
31	UNSC membership from 15 to 24 by 5per/4nonper	31	-0.774
15	Membership of UNSC increase from 15 to 25 6per/4nonper	15	-0.808
4	Germany ready to shoulder resps with UNSC membership	4	-0.941
32	4 new nonper 1 Afr, 1 Asi, 1 Eas.Eu, 1 LatAm	32	-1.120
28	Permanent not belong into constit as noting permanent	28	-1.341
23	veto action against breach of in law not accept	23	-2.130

PQMethod2.35 UNSC Reform - Germany/United States PAGE 7
Path and Project Name: C:\PQMethod\projects/UNSCRE Jul 12 16

Descending Array of Differences Between Factors 1 and 2

No.	Statement	No.	Type 1	Type 2	Difference
23	veto action against breach of in law not accept	23	0.945	-2.130	3.075
4	Germany ready to shoulder resps with UNSC membership	4	1.422	-0.941	2.363
16	State who has ressources should have incfluence	16	1.262	-0.516	1.778
13	SC capability increase when members with contribu J/D	13	1.204	-0.394	1.598
31	UNSC membership from 15 to 24 by 5per/4nonper	31	0.743	-0.774	1.516
8	Alongside geographical distrib, contributions should mem	8	1.706	0.226	1.480
32	4 new nonper 1 Afr, 1 Asi, 1 Eas.Eu, 1 LatAm	32	0.193	-1.120	1.313
15	Membership of UNSC increase from 15 to 25 6per/4nonper	15	0.465	-0.808	1.273
12	Current SC setting unable to appease or prevent conflict	12	0.667	-0.480	1.146
7	US interests depend on behavior, criteria-based approach	7	0.957	-0.118	1.075
9	When SC legislates, sets rules for all UN	9	0.468	-0.420	0.888
19	Germany has always taken EU interest into account	19	0.465	-0.113	0.578
20	Major advan of G4 rest on fair geog rep	20	-0.039	-0.552	0.513
28	Permanent not belong into constit as noting permanent	28	-1.397	-1.341	-0.056
29	Not surpirsing that UNSC reform is called for	29	-0.196	-0.075	-0.122
22	veto has widenend gap between devel/non devel world	22	-0.939	-0.726	-0.213
26	Idea of UNSC ref support from US to make J/D members	26	-0.646	-0.265	-0.381
3	US supports expan without diminish effec or effiec	3	0.480	0.877	-0.397
21	40 years after estab, reform is desirable	21	-0.266	0.168	-0.434
27	Global north is perm outvoted by South	27	-0.465	0.086	-0.551
2	Unlike J/D BRIC vote contrary US showing bilat not coop	2	0.200	0.871	-0.671
5	Modification of veto meets resistance of P5	5	1.489	2.189	-0.701
11	US open in princip to limited enlargement of UNSC	11	0.015	0.789	-0.774
18	UNSC debate is about geopolitics but also int sec	18	-0.027	0.835	-0.862
10	UN may be multilat but world ruled by US	10	-1.669	-0.690	-0.980
24	To keep UN under auth US is in arrears of payments	24	-1.241	-0.201	-1.040
30	Reference to Germany as contrib is Machtpolitik	30	-1.292	-0.235	-1.057
25	Too much to lose in UNSC reform to make it realpol	25	-1.436	-0.140	-1.297
14	Debate in UNGA caused competition for multilateralism	14	-1.187	0.516	-1.702
6	For US idea enlargement is G4	6	-0.532	1.400	-1.932
1	US not open enlarge by CH amend changes veto	1	0.513	2.606	-2.093
17	There should be no changes to veto	17	-1.860	1.475	-3.334

PQMethod2.35 UNSC Reform - Germany/United States PAGE 8
Path and Project Name: C:\PQMethod\projects/UNSCRE Jul 12 16

Exact Factor Scores (á la SPSS) in Z-Score and T-Score units

No.	Statement	No.	Factors 1		2	
1	US not open enlarge by CH amend changes veto	1	0.35	54	2.63	76
2	Unlike J/D BRIC vote contrary US showing bilat not coo	2	0.30	53	0.87	59
3	US supports expan without diminish effec or effiec	3	0.78	58	0.96	60
4	Germany ready to shoulder resps with UNSC membership	4	1.74	67	-1.02	40
5	Modification of veto meets resistance of P5	5	1.52	65	2.33	73
6	For US idea enlargement is G4	6	-0.66	43	1.01	60
7	US interests depend on behavior, criteria-based approa	7	0.89	59	-0.22	48
8	Alongside geographical distrib, contributions should m	8	1.73	67	-0.07	49
9	When SC legislates, sets rules for all UN	9	0.32	53	-0.42	46
10	UN may be multilat but world ruled by US	10	-1.87	31	-0.80	42
11	US open in princip to limited enlargement of UNSC	11	0.32	53	0.86	59
12	Current SC setting unable to appease or prevent confli	12	0.28	53	-0.54	45
13	SC capability increase when members with contribu J/D	13	1.04	60	-0.45	45
14	Debate in UNGA caused competition for multilateralism	14	-1.22	38	0.39	54
15	Membership of UNSC increase from 15 to 25 6per/4nonper	15	0.78	58	-0.94	41
16	State who has ressources should have incfluence	16	1.17	62	-0.75	42
17	There should be no changes to veto	17	-1.51	35	1.53	65
18	UNSC debate is about geopolitics but also int sec	18	-0.06	49	0.91	59
19	Germany has always taken EU interest into account	19	0.25	52	-0.07	49
20	Major advan of G4 rest on fair geog rep	20	0.09	51	-0.35	46
21	40 years after estab, reform is desirable	21	-0.27	47	0.04	50
22	veto has widenend gap between devel/non devel world	22	-1.03	40	-0.89	41
23	veto action against breach of in law not accept	23	0.49	55	-1.83	32
24	To keep UN under auth US is in arrears of payments	24	-1.58	34	-0.02	50
25	Too much to lose in UNSC reform to make it realpol	25	-1.55	35	0.25	52
26	Idea of UNSC ref support from US to make J/D members	26	-0.16	48	0.02	50
27	Global north is perm outvoted by South	27	-0.51	45	-0.04	50
28	Permanent not belong into constit as noting permanent	28	-1.07	39	-1.52	35
29	Not surpirsing that UNSC reform is called for	29	-0.26	47	-0.03	50
30	Reference to Germany as contrib is Machtpolitik	30	-1.21	38	-0.17	48
31	UNSC membership from 15 to 24 by 5per/4nonper	31	0.84	58	-0.86	41
32	4 new nonper 1 Afr, 1 Asi, 1 Eas.Eu, 1 LatAm	32	0.06	51	-0.79	42

PQMethod2.35 UNSC Reform - Germany/United States PAGE 9
Path and Project Name: C:\PQMethod\projects/UNSCRE Jul 12 16

Factor Q-Sort Values for Each Statement

No.	Statement	No.	Factor Arrays 1	2
1	US not open enlarge by CH amend changes veto	1	1	4
2	Unlike J/D BRIC vote contrary US showing bilat not coop	2	0	2
3	US supports expan without diminish effec or effiec	3	1	2
4	Germany ready to shoulder resps with UNSC membership	4	3	-2
5	Modification of veto meets resistance of P5	5	3	3
6	For US idea enlargement is G4	6	-1	2
7	US interests depend on behavior, criteria-based approach	7	2	0
8	Alongside geographical distrib, contributions should mem	8	4	1
9	When SC legislates, sets rules for all UN	9	1	-1
10	UN may be multilat but world ruled by US	10	-3	-1
11	US open in princip to limited enlargement of UNSC	11	0	1
12	Current SC setting unable to appease or prevent conflict	12	1	-1
13	SC capability increase when members with contribu J/D	13	2	0
14	Debate in UNGA caused competition for multilateralism	14	-2	1
15	Membership of UNSC increase from 15 to 25 6per/4nonper	15	0	-2
16	State who has ressources should have incfluence	16	2	-1
17	There should be no changes to veto	17	-4	3
18	UNSC debate is about geopolitics but also int sec	18	0	2
19	Germany has always taken EU interest into account	19	0	0
20	Major advan of G4 rest on fair geog rep	20	0	-1
21	40 years after estab, reform is desirable	21	-1	1
22	veto has widenend gap between devel/non devel world	22	-1	-2
23	veto action against breach of in law not accept	23	2	-4
24	To keep UN under auth US is in arrears of payments	24	-2	0
25	Too much to lose in UNSC reform to make it realpol	25	-3	0
26	Idea of UNSC ref support from US to make J/D members	26	-1	0
27	Global north is perm outvoted by South	27	-1	1
28	Permanent not belong into constit as noting permanent	28	-2	-3
29	Not surpirsing that UNSC reform is called for	29	0	0
30	Reference to Germany as contrib is Machtpolitik	30	-2	0
31	UNSC membership from 15 to 24 by 5per/4nonper	31	1	-2
32	4 new nonper 1 Afr, 1 Asi, 1 Eas.Eu, 1 LatAm	32	0	-3

Variance = 3.438 St. Dev. = 1.854

PQMethod2.35 UNSC Reform - Germany/United States PAGE 10
Path and Project Name: C:\PQMethod\projects/UNSCRE Jul 12 16

Factor Q-Sort Values for Statements sorted by Consensus vs. Disagreement (Variance across Factor Z-Scores)

No.	Statement	No.	Factor Arrays 1	2
28	Permanent not belong into constit as noting permanent	28	-2	-3
29	Not surpirsing that UNSC reform is called for	29	0	0
22	veto has widenend gap between devel/non devel world	22	-1	-2
26	Idea of UNSC ref support from US to make J/D members	26	-1	0
3	US supports expan without diminish effec or effiec	3	1	2
21	40 years after estab, reform is desirable	21	-1	1
20	Major advan of G4 rest on fair geog rep	20	0	-1
27	Global north is perm outvoted by South	27	-1	1
19	Germany has always taken EU interest into account	19	0	0
2	Unlike J/D BRIC vote contrary US showing bilat not coop	2	0	2
5	Modification of veto meets resistance of P5	5	3	3
11	US open in princip to limited enlargement of UNSC	11	0	1
18	UNSC debate is about geopolitics but also int sec	18	0	2
9	When SC legislates, sets rules for all UN	9	1	-1
10	UN may be multilat but world ruled by US	10	-3	-1
24	To keep UN under auth US is in arrears of payments	24	-2	0
30	Reference to Germany as contrib is Machtpolitik	30	-2	0
7	US interests depend on behavior, criteria-based approach	7	2	0
12	Current SC setting unable to appease or prevent conflict	12	1	-1
15	Membership of UNSC increase from 15 to 25 6per/4nonper	15	0	-2
25	Too much to lose in UNSC reform to make it realpol	25	-3	0
32	4 new nonper 1 Afr, 1 Asi, 1 Eas.Eu, 1 LatAm	32	0	-3
8	Alongside geographical distrib, contributions should mem	8	4	1
31	UNSC membership from 15 to 24 by 5per/4nonper	31	1	-2
13	SC capability increase when members with contribu J/D	13	2	0
14	Debate in UNGA caused competition for multilateralism	14	-2	1
16	State who has ressources should have incfluence	16	2	-1
6	For US idea enlargement is G4	6	-1	2
1	US not open enlarge by CH amend changes veto	1	1	4
4	Germany ready to shoulder resps with UNSC membership	4	3	-2
23	veto action against breach of in law not accept	23	2	-4
17	There should be no changes to veto	17	-4	3

PQMethod2.35 UNSC Reform - Germany/United States PAGE 11
Path and Project Name: C:\PQMethod\projects/UNSCRE Jul 12 16

Factor Characteristics

	Factors 1	2
No. of Defining Variables	5	4
Average Rel. Coef.	0.800	0.800
Composite Reliability	0.952	0.941
S.E. of Factor Z-Scores	0.218	0.243

Standard Errors for Differences in Factor Z-Scores

(Diagonal Entries Are S.E. Within Factors)

Factors	1	2
1	0.309	0.326
2	0.326	0.343

PQMethod2.35 UNSC Reform - Germany/United States PAGE 12
Path and Project Name: C:\PQMethod\projects/UNSCRE Jul 12 16

Distinguishing Statements for Factor 1

(P < .05 ; Asterisk (*) Indicates Significance at P < .01)

Both the Factor Q-Sort Value (Q-SV) and the Z-Score (Z-SCR) are Shown.

No.	Statement	No.	Factors 1 Q-SV	1 Z-SCR	2 Q-SV	2 Z-SCR
8	Alongside geographical distrib, contributions should mem	8	4	1.71*	1	0.23
5	Modification of veto meets resistance of P5	5	3	1.49	3	2.19
4	Germany ready to shoulder resps with UNSC membership	4	3	1.42*	-2	-0.94
16	State who has ressources should have incfluence	16	2	1.26*	-1	-0.52
13	SC capability increase when members with contribu J/D	13	2	1.20*	0	-0.39
7	US interests depend on behavior, criteria-based approach	7	2	0.96*	0	-0.12
23	veto action against breach of in law not accept	23	2	0.94*	-4	-2.13
31	UNSC membership from 15 to 24 by 5per/4nonper	31	1	0.74*	-2	-0.77
12	Current SC setting unable to appease or prevent conflict	12	1	0.67*	-1	-0.48
1	US not open enlarge by CH amend changes veto	1	1	0.51*	4	2.61
9	When SC legislates, sets rules for all UN	9	1	0.47*	-1	-0.42
15	Membership of UNSC increase from 15 to 25 6per/4nonper	15	0	0.46*	-2	-0.81
2	Unlike J/D BRIC vote contrary US showing bilat not coop	2	0	0.20	2	0.87
32	4 new nonper 1 Afr, 1 Asi, 1 Eas.Eu, 1 LatAm	32	0	0.19*	-3	-1.12
11	US open in princip to limited enlargement of UNSC	11	0	0.02	1	0.79
18	UNSC debate is about geopolitics but also int sec	18	0	-0.03*	2	0.83
6	For US idea enlargement is G4	6	-1	-0.53*	2	1.40
14	Debate in UNGA caused competition for multilateralism	14	-2	-1.19*	1	0.52
24	To keep UN under auth US is in arrears of payments	24	-2	-1.24*	0	-0.20
30	Reference to Germany as contrib is Machtpolitik	30	-2	-1.29*	0	-0.24
25	Too much to lose in UNSC reform to make it realpol	25	-3	-1.44*	0	-0.14
10	UN may be multilat but world ruled by US	10	-3	-1.67*	-1	-0.69
17	There should be no changes to veto	17	-4	-1.86*	3	1.47

PQMethod2.35 UNSC Reform - Germany/United States PAGE 13
Path and Project Name: C:\PQMethod\projects/UNSCRE Jul 12 16

Consensus Statements -- Those That Do Not Distinguish Between ANY Pair of Factors.

All Listed Statements are Non-Significant at P>.01, and Those Flagged With an * are also Non-Significant at P>.05.

			Factors			
			1		2	
No.	Statement	No.	Q-SV	Z-SCR	Q-SV	Z-SCR
2	Unlike J/D BRIC vote contrary US showing bilat not coop	2	0	0.20	2	0.87
3*	US supports expan without diminish effec or effiec	3	1	0.48	2	0.88
5	Modification of veto meets resistance of P5	5	3	1.49	3	2.19
11	US open in princip to limited enlargement of UNSC	11	0	0.02	1	0.79
19*	Germany has always taken EU interest into account	19	0	0.46	0	-0.11
20*	Major advan of G4 rest on fair geog rep	20	0	-0.04	-1	-0.55
21*	40 years after estab, reform is desirable	21	-1	-0.27	1	0.17
22*	veto has widenend gap between devel/non devel world	22	-1	-0.94	-2	-0.73
26*	Idea of UNSC ref support from US to make J/D members	26	-1	-0.65	0	-0.27
27*	Global north is perm outvoted by South	27	-1	-0.46	1	0.09
28*	Permanent not belong into constit as noting permanent	28	-2	-1.40	-3	-1.34
29*	Not surpirsing that UNSC reform is called for	29	0	-0.20	0	-0.07

QANALYZE was completet at 22:36:26

About the author

Andreas Schwenk was born in Essen, Germany and works as a consultant at the crossroads of politics and communications with a focus on nation branding, campaign management and crisis communications. His academic interests include international relations, foreign policy and public relations. Schwenk holds a Master of Science Degree in Public Administration (Leiden University, The Netherlands) and a Master of Science Degree in Strategic Communications & Public Relations (University of Stirling, United Kingdom & Pompeu Fabra University, Spain).

Zeitfracht Medien GmbH
Ferdinand-Jühlke-Straße 7
99095 Erfurt, Deutschland
produktsicherheit@kolibri360.de